THE KAMORO

New Guinea Communications

Volume 10

KAL MULLER

THE KAMORO

NEW GUINEA COMMUNICATIONS

Volume 10

GALDA VERLAG 2022

ISBN 978-3-96203-223-4 (Print)
ISBN 978-3-96203-224-1 (Ebook)

Bibliografische Information der Deutschen Nationalbibliothek
Die Deutsche Nationalbibliothek verzeichnet diese Publikation in der Deutschen
Nationalbibliografie; detaillierte bibliografische Daten sind im Internet über
http://dnb.ddb.de abrufbar.

© 2022 Galda Verlag, Glienicke
Neither this book nor any part may be reproduced or transmitted in any form or by any means
electronic or mechanical, including photocopying, micro-filming, and recording, or by any
information storage or retrieval system, without prior permission in writing from the publisher.
Direct all inquiries to Galda Verlag, Franz-Schubert-Str. 61, 16548 Glienicke, Germany

KAMORO
THE MIMIKA TRIBE

The Kamoro were initially called the Mimika by outsiders. This name was based on a large river that ran through their territory. They live on the south coast of West New Guinea. Then in the 1930s, Father Drabbe, a Roman Catholic missionary and linguist, found that this group called themselves Kamoro. In their language, this word means '*all humans alive*' as opposed to deceased humans, ghosts, spirits, not objects, plants and animals. So, this term could be applied to all humans alive on earth today. The word establishes a relation with the ancestors' world of the deceased, along with their mythical cultural heroes.

In an alternate explanation, the use of the appellation Kamoro could perhaps also have begun during their first contact with the outside world. They might have been asked: 'What do you call yourselves?' And the reply could have been 'Kamoro', we who are alive, and they have been known by this name ever since. Almost all the literature about them uses this term and they have accepted it as an old misunderstanding that is too late to correct.

Some Kamoro have maintained to me that the correct name for themselves is '*Mimika-we*'. This term literally means 'the people of the muddy river'. And indeed, a large, muddy river called Mimika runs through their lands.

The Kamoro claim that their territory runs 'from Potawai to Nakai'. This is not very accurate. Potowai Buru is the westernmost Kamoro village in the Mimika District (Kabupaten Mimika). But there are three Kamoro-speaking villages further west. The farthest is Warifi Village on Teluk (Bay) Lakahia/ Etna. To the east, Kamoro-land ends near Timika, with the lands of the Nawaripi Village. A different language group called Sempan lives to the east, and farther yet, Nakai is an Asmat village. So, if we take language as the criterion for defining the territory of the Kamoro, their spread should be designated as 'from Warifi to Nawaripi'.

PREFACE

The Kamoro occupy a long stretch of coast along the northern shore of the Arafura Sea and a short distance inland. Its westernmost section was connected to the trade network of eastern Indonesia with its sources of power on the islands of Ternate and Tidore. The western section of Kamoroland bore the brunt of occasional deadly attacks by the Asmat who lived further down the coast, past a stretch of uninhabited mangrove swamps. Until backed by Dutch firearms, the Kamoro were no match for the fierce Asmat warriors. Many a Kamoro head ended up in an Asmat longhouse.

Fate and geology deposited a huge gold and copper ore body inland from the Kamoro homeland. An American mining company, Freeport Indonesia, eventually began to build its infrastructure for its first mine in the late 1960s. The company's first airport, port and road all began in the eastern part of the Kamoro territory. While obtaining little help initially, the Kamoro in this area later profited greatly from Freeport's social programs.

From the mid-1990s to the late 2010s, I participated in some of Freeport's programs that benefited the Kamoro. I was impressed by the fine wood carvings of this group, in many cases as good as that of the Asmat, their far better-known neighbors. I developed a program of purchasing and marketing of Kamoro art, for Bali, Jakarta, as well as for the mine's company staff and personnel in Tembagapura, in West New Guinea.

In a previous book in this series, we covered the main cultures in southern West New Guinea. These include the Marind, the Kimaam Islanders, the Asmat, and the Sempan as well the Kamoro. This book complements and amplifies the information on this group.

I did not use footnotes and not all sources are identified in the text. For those wishing more information, we provide a complete bibliography.

In this book, we refer to the Indonesian half of the island as West New Guinea. This is to distinguish it from Papua New Guinea (PNG) an independent country that covers the eastern half of the island. The western half was originally called Netherlands New Guinea, then Irian Barat, and also Irian Jaya under Indonesian rule. In 2001 the name Papua was used for this area. Then in 2003 this half of the island was split into two provinces, one called Papua, the other West Papua. The indigenous inhabitants of this area who want to become independent prefer the name West Papua, but this can cause confusion with the same name for one of the provinces. Whence our choice: West New Guinea.

CONTENTS

KAMORO: The Mimika Tribe	*v*
Preface	*vii*
Table of contents	*ix*
Introduction	*xiii*

1 Background 1

The most remote ancestors 5

The Kamoro language:
how it fits into the larger picture 6

Kamoro myths 9

2 Social Structure 11

Effects on the environment 13

The 'paraeko' 14

The 'taparu' 15

The village 17

3 Early Kamoro Contacts with the Outside World 21

First contacts with Europeans 24

Events since the 1850s 27

4 The Kamoro 100 Years Ago: The British Ornithological Union Expedition 33

Canoes 35

Dwellings and settlements 36

Clothing 37

Rituals and art 39

Fishing and weapons 41

Disposal of the dead 43

Expedition problems and final opinions.................. 45

5 The Dutch Government, the Roman Catholic Mission and WWII: Drastic Changes 47

Changes in Kamoro lives 51

Asmat raids 55

A hydroplane base in Kamoro-land 55

World War II 56

6 The Post-WWII Period 61

Changes in the Roman Catholic Church 63

The Protestants try again. 67

Evolution of Kamoro attitudes 68

Freeport and the Kamoro: encouraging carving ... 70

7 Kamoro Rituals 75

Kamoro initiation: Father Zegwaard 81

8 The Karapao Today 85

9 Kamoro Art:
Revival , Evolution And Commercialization 95

Reviving Kamoro art 99

Types of Kamoro art made today 99

Kamoro lifestyle, markets, problems and needs:
the role of carvings 111

The tools of the trade 114

Kinds of wood used 115

10 The Yearly Kamoro Kakuru Festival 117

Freeport contributions 121

Out to the villages: spreading the news 121

The festival's changing locations 123

Problems 125

The following festivals 127

The auctions 129

Positive aspects of the festival 133

The bottom-line: why the festival was canceled 136

11 Picking Kamoro Art... 139

Criteria for Kamoro art purchases........................... 143

Resurrection and new creation 147

Choosing carvings for the yearly festival.................. 148

Choosing carvings for exhibits/sales........................ 150

The Kamoro Art Gallery 152

12 Taking carvers out of West New Guinea........................ 155

Exposition in Holland 159

An emotional visit... 160

Daily activities 161

Carvings and the auction.. 163

The end of the Leiden Kamoro exposition:
disappointments... 166

BIBLIOGRAPHY 167

INTRODUCTION

This book about the Kamoro highlights their history and ethnography. I hope to give a long-term perspective on this ethnolinguistic group. To accomplish this, I draw on previously published material on the Kamoro as well as my personal experience.

The target audience for this book includes people interested in West New Guinea as well as all Papuans, and especially the Kamoro. A body of literature (see our bibliography) already exists on the Kamoro, but many gaps need to be filled. And many of the books in the bibliography are difficult to obtain and expensive, I have combined my 20 years of experience with the Kamoro with the information available in the published literature.

However, much more needs to be done for a better understanding of this fascinating culture. And this needs to be accomplished relatively quickly as many of the older men who still remember almost-forgotten aspects of their culture, will not live much longer. Of course, a Kamoro would best record the saving of this important knowledge, but a qualified outsider, willing to learn the language, could do so as well. Although not many young Kamoro are currently interested in their traditional culture, this will hopefully change in the future, and material must be gathered and analyzed now before it is too late.

I am not an anthropologist, nor did I learn to speak the Kamoro language. All my communications with the Kamoro were in Indonesian. Nor did I live for any extended periods in any single Kamoro village. Thus, I never acquired the necessary level of understanding to delve deeply into this culture. My first-hand knowledge has perforce remained relatively superficial. I have had to supplement this with extensive use of texts by specialists, especially by the anthropologist Dr. Jan Pouwer and Roman Catholic priests. I was personally

The southern coast of West New Guinea is cut by many rivers that meander once they reach the lowlands from the high central mountains. The Kamoro live along these rivers and the coast of the Arafura Sea where the rivers end.

very involved in the material covered in several chapters, especially Chapter 10 (The Yearly Kamoro Festival) and Chapter 11 (Picking Kamoro Art).

Between 1995 and 2017 I frequently visited the Kamoro and worked with them in the promotion and marketing of their carvings. The mining company, Freeport Indonesia, wholly supported this work. I designed and carried out this program with several purposes in mind. First and foremost, I wanted to help the Kamoro to keep alive their carving tradition, often as good as that of the much better-known Asmat. I hoped that through this program the Kamoro would acquire a sense of pride in their traditions and revive some aspects that had been almost forgotten. I also tried to interest the outside world in the Kamoro culture by taking visitors to Kamoro villages and bringing small groups of Kamoro to Holland, Jakarta and Bali to carve and perform dances at schools and exhibitions.

Combining the old and the new, a Kamoro stands beside a motorcycle while wearing traditional finery. His headdress is made of cassowary feathers and his torso is covered with white paint from burnt and crushed seashells.

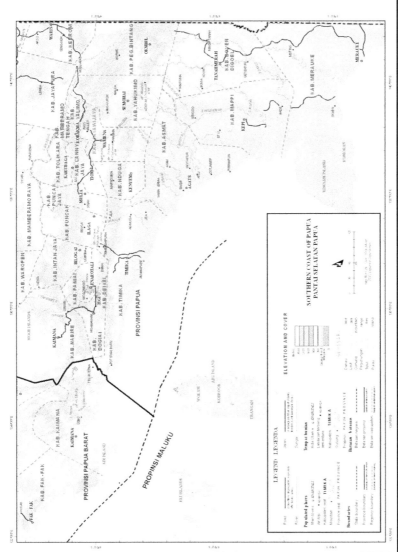

The Kamoro lands encompass a broad area between the island's central mountains and the Arafura Sea. The Kamoro live in the stretch between Etna Bay and to just east of the town of Timika where the Sempan lands begin.

BACKGROUND

1

The ancestors of the Kamoro settled by the Arafura Sea that separates Australia from southern West New Guinea. Families from inland villages often set up camps by the sea to fish and gather seafood.

The Kamoro live on a 250-kilometer stretch of the south coast, between Etna Bay in the west and the Minajerwi (Muamiua) River to the east. Starting at Etna Bay in the west, their territory reaches just beyond the town of Timika. The group holds about 18,000 individuals, scattered among some 40 villages. Most of these villages are located on the coast, with a half-dozen found inland where the mountains are further from the Arafura Sea. Each Kamoro village is located next to a river.

Since the 1970s, many Kamoro have moved to the vicinity of Timika, living in town or various transmigration settlements. Well over 1,000 of them live on Pulau Keraka, located in front of Freeport's docks at Amamapare. Many Kamoro have moved out from their villages for access to better educational and health facilities as well as for selling fish and paid employment.

Except for a few government officials and missionaries, the Kamoro did not attract much attention from the outside world until the early 1970s when the giant international mining company, Freeport Indonesia, built its basic infrastructure. Its main port, Amamapare lies near the coast, and its landing strip was built next to what is now Timika town. This infrastructure, including a part of the connecting road from the port to the mine area in the highlands, was built on the eastern portion of traditionally Kamoro-owned land. The Amungme, who live just to the north of the Kamoro, claim all the land to where the stones stop in the Ajkwa River, with considerable overlap with what the Kamoro consider as theirs. In the old days, this overlap area was a no-man's land, where both groups did some hunting. With the Freeport infrastructure and the towns of Timika and Kuala Kencana, this 'overlap-land' has become extremely valuable. Non-Papuans now hold legal titles to a considerable proportion that the central government has claimed as state-owned.

The presence of Freeport Indonesia also began to attract a degree of ethnographic attention to the Kamoro. The company sponsored a book, *Kamoro: Between the Tides in Irian Jaya* by David Pickell. A young American anthropologist, Todd Harple, worked for Freeport and gathered material on the Kamoro through interviews, as he did not live in any Kamoro villages. After the company terminated his employment, he wrote a dissertation to obtain his PhD in 2000 at the Australian National University: *Controlling the Dragon: An ethnohistorical analysis of the Kamoro of Southwest New Guinea*. Then starting in 1998, thanks to Freeport sponsorship, I organized a series of

Mapurupiu was an important cultural hero to the Kamoro, so important that a statue was erected in his memory. His legend includes many travails but also credits him with the invention of the canoe. In one version he was helped by a frog, whilst a modern version credits him for the invention of the outboard engine.

yearly Kamoro festivals that began a serious revival of some items of Kamoro carvings and traditional practices. A Belgian anthropologist, Karen Jacobs, attended several of these festivals and wrote her 2003 doctoral dissertation on the history of collecting Kamoro art: *Collecting Kamoro* which she published as a book in 2011.

The most remote ancestors

The ancestors of the Kamoro, like those of all Papuans and other Homo sapiens, first left eastern Africa around 60,000 years ago. As part of this migration, the first Papuans arrived on the island of New Guinea some 50,000 years ago. They traveled from the west, having made their way across the Indonesian archipelago, perhaps using bamboo rafts for crossing the sea passages between islands. This was no mass migration, but small groups of a few families arriving over probably several thousand years. The ancestors of Australia's aborigines arrived from the same direction during the same timeframe. At times during the Ice Ages, southern West New Guinea, the Kamoro homeland, and northern Australia were connected by land when the Arafura Sea dried up. (Pawley, 2005) The final separation of West New Guinea from Australia occurred some 8 to 10,000 years ago. This was a long enough timespan for the two somewhat different physical types, Papuan and Australian Aboriginal, to have evolved.

The early Papuans lived on the seashore, collecting various types of edible mollusks, and probably fishing, and hunting as well. As the climate began warming after the last glacial period, Papuans started to make their way inland, into the mountains, to hunt and collect pandanus and other nuts. Incipient agriculture began some 9,000 years ago in the highlands, and perhaps even earlier in the lowlands. The main plants domesticated were yam and taro tubers, along with bananas and sugar cane. As the climate warmed, Papuans spread to all areas in the highlands capable of supporting agriculture.

We can only infer the history of the Kamoro from the physical and climatic changes in the environment in West New Guinea. There are no written records about the Kamoro until the arrival of the first Europeans and those accounts are very much one-sided, as we do not know how the Kamoro felt about the Europeans. From the Kamoro, we have only myths and legends that might hold a grain of truth, but cannot be relied on as accurate history.

But there is one field that can help us to understand how the Kamoro fit into the cultures of Papua: linguistics.

The Kamoro language: how it fits into the larger picture

The Kamoro language has six mutually understandable dialects. (Drabbe, 1953) However, mysteriously, a single village, called Kaugapu, speaks a language that seems completely different, unintelligible to the rest of the Kamoro. Their tongue is a part of the Kamoro-Asmat language family that also includes the Sempan who live between these two larger groups. The eastern Sempan resemble the Kamoro in some ways, while the western Sempan are more similar with the Asmat.

How does the Kamoro language fit in with the others in West New Guinea? And what can it tell us about past migrations? To attempt an answer to these questions, we must look at some basic linguistics. All the languages in West New Guinea are divided into two major groups: the far older Papuan languages, called Non-Austronesian (NAN) and the more recent Malayo-Polynesian (or Austronesian AN). The roots of the Papuan NAN languages date back to the first human settlements on the island of New Guinea, some 500 centuries back.

The speakers of Malayo-Polynesian arrived considerably later, probably around 3,500 to 4,000 years ago. These 'recent' arrivals settled among the Papuans, along the north coast of New Guinea and offshore islands in both PNG and West New Guinea. In the west, they established themselves mostly on the island of Cenderawasih Bay (Biak and Yapen), along the north coast, the Raja Ampat islands and in pockets along the coast between Bintuni Bay and Etna Bay. Just to the west of Etna Bay, along the coast, the Kowiai language belongs to this group. Kaimana is located in this area. Inland, to the west of Etna Bay, we find the Semini and the Mairasi, both Papuan language groups. These two groups separate the Kamoro from the Kemberau and the Buruwai, who live around the lower half of the large, convoluted Arguni Bay. (Silzer, 1991) These two groups belong, according to linguists, to the same general language group as the Kamoro and the Asmat. So, at one time they may have all been located in one area, prior to their dispersal.

There are many more Papuan languages spoken on the island of New Guinea than the different Malayo-Polynesian ones. The Papuan languages are divided into three major groups called phyla (whose singular is phylum).

These are the Trans-New Guinea Phylum, the West Papuan (Bird's Head) Phylum and the Geelvink (Cenderawasih) Bay Phylum. The first of these holds, by far, the greatest number of languages. All the central highlands languages as well as those of the southeast coast, including the Kamoro-Sempan-Asmat, belong to this Trans-New Guinea Phylum.

To the east of the Kamoro homeland, the little-known group, the Sempan, occupy a large territory. Immediately to the east of the Sempan, the well-known Asmat spread out both along the coast and inland. We have no information on the south coast groups to the west of the Kamoro. There are nine different linguistic groups between Etna Bay and Bintuni Bay. Dr. Jan Pouwer (Pouwer, 1955) wrote that there were similarities between the Kamoro and the tribes to the west, but we can provide no further information, except for the linguistics mentioned above. To the north, the Amungme live in the mountainous highlands. To the south, the Arafura Sea lies between the Kamoro area and northern Australia.

The Kamoro probably first arrived in their present homeland from the east. Their language and culture have a number of similarities with the Asmat and there are legends of migration from the east to the west. Some (slight) indications from linguistics and art styles point to a possible migration from the north coast of New Guinea. This could be either the area of Lake Sentani or the Sepik River. But there is no definite evidence for these possible places of origin for the Kamoro.

The geography of the southeast coast of West New Guinea has changed considerably during the past 20,000 years. During an early period, at the height of the last Ice Age, sea levels were some 120 meters lower than today. This meant that the shallow Arafura Sea did not exist at that time, with New Guinea and Australia forming a single landmass. Humans could have walked and lived in the area now covered by the Arafura Sea. Then, as the world's temperature increased, the sea level rose due to melting ice, until the Arafura Sea was formed and isolated the landmasses of New Guinea and Australia from each other, some 8,000 years ago, separated by the Torres Strait.

Then, a large segment of the south coast of New Guinea called the Fly-Digul Platform took shape due to geological forces called 'tectonic downwarping'.

The sea level was up to four meters higher than at present in places. The western half of this platform includes the area now occupied by the Asmat-Kamoro language family. But when the area was underwater, of course, there could not have been any humans living there. The current

*Ancestral spirits are represented in wood carvings called '**wemawe**'. They are made today for sale, mostly to foreign visitors and Freeport mine workers.*

shoreline and the sea level date from some 6,000 years ago, due to sedimentation from south-flowing rivers and a re-adjustment of the earth's crust. (Pawley, 2005)

This fits in neatly with the current theory of the relatively late settlement of the region by Papuans of the Trans-New Guinea Phylum. The probable date of the settlement of this area of the south coast of West New Guinea was only some 3,000 years ago. The groups now found in the southeast area of West New Guinea migrated south from the central mountain range when conditions allowed them to do so. One proof of this resides in some (slight) similarities between the languages of the Asmat-Kamoro and that of the mountain Ok. Additional evidence comes from Kamoro myths and legends, all of which point to the east as their ancestral home prior to migrating to their current homeland.

Kamoro myths

Sometime after contact began with the outside world, Kamoro myths and legends came to accommodate and incorporate foreigners and their cultural items. We are most fortunate in the fact that three Dutch missionary-linguists, Fathers Drabbe, Coenen and Zegwaard, recorded many Kamoro myths. There are several different versions of these myths. Names are spelt differently, and details vary, but the core meanings stay comparable. We do not have space here to go into depth into these legends, but there will be some general comments on understanding the Kamoro culture and psychology. (For *Amoko*, a book of Kamoro myths, see Offenberg, 2002.)

As everywhere in the world, religion gives followers a measure of psychological security, especially useful when facing illness, death and other human or natural disasters. Myths combine cosmology with the fundamentals of religion. Kamoro cosmology separates the upper and more important lower world, placing humans in between them.

Many believe that the supernatural affects human lives, and this can at least be partially controlled through religion, bringing a degree of safety and assurance. Rituals often find their bases in myths, believed to be facts by the followers of any religion. This holds true for the great worldwide monotheistic religions as well as the traditional ones.

The Kamoro believe that their cultural heroes the '*amoko*' (as their adventures are depicted in myths) created everyone on earth and everything in it. Modern versions of these myths include items such as motorboats, rifles and cloth, which were introduced by outsiders, very obviously not Kamoro inventions.

One widespread Kamoro myth concerns a dragon (or a huge snake) that today is sometimes called a Komodo dragon. Perhaps it is based on an even larger lizard that died out in Australia perhaps some 20,000 years ago. Be that as it may, a particular dragon ate all humans except a pregnant woman. She gave birth to a son, Mbiro-koteyau, who eventually slew the dragon. After this feat, he cut open the dragon and its various parts became all the human races found on earth. Thus, all mankind originated thanks to this Kamoro cultural hero, spreading from Kamoro lands. (Coenen, 1963) (Drabbe, 1947-1950) (Offenberg, 2002)

The ancestors of the Europeans, the Chinese and the Indonesians all left Kamoro-land to settle in the west. This was also the case for many Kamoro male and female cultural heroes who traveled to the west, most of them never to return. But some of their descendants eventually did come back to the area of their first ancestors.

In another legend, an old man named Mapurupiu died. His soul wanders in search of other souls, in the land of the dead. As he rested on his journey, he found a frog (in some versions also a snake) that made a canoe for him. In later versions of the same myth, the canoe was equipped with an outboard motor by the frog. This is an example of how 'modern' inventions are incorporated into old legends. Some authors have equated Mapurupiu with the biblical Adam, apparently the first human. Another interpretation holds Mapurupiu as an all-powerful God who punished mankind for their sins with death. In the original legend, Mapurupiu killed his brother. This was because his younger brother did not bother to fulfil all his funerary obligations and married Mapurupiu's widow far too soon. Aside from discovering how to make canoes, this hero laid down many of the rules of Kamoro life. (Offenberg, 2002)

Many Kamoro, especially in the eastern and central areas, consider Mapurupiu as the ultimate cultural hero. Due to this, a tall monument was erected in his honor in 2006, near the present-day village of Mware. Aside from discovering how to make canoes, this hero laid down many of the rules of Kamoro life.

The bark of the 'massoy' tree was an important export from the Kamoro area in pre-European times. It is still exported to Java for folk medicines and as a color fixative for batik cloth.

SOCIAL STRUCTURE 2

Birds-of-paradise were hunted by the Kamoro and exchanged with merchants for metal tools and cloth. These birds were exported after their legs were cut off, leading Europeans to believe that they lived with no feet.

Kamoro social life expands outward from the basic nuclear family: father, mother, and their children. The former prevailing matriarchy has been fading since the arrival of the Roman Catholic Church and government, Dutch, then Indonesian. These outside forces, based on patriarchies, dominated the Kamoro and continue to impose their values. The former matriarchy survives, barely if at all, in small groupings called '*peraeko*'. Various '*peraeko*' are grouped into '*taparu*', a term sometimes translated as clan, that united in the past to make up the villages. A wider circle includes each of the six dialect (mutually comprehensible) groups, and finally the encompassing term Kamoro that applies to all those who speak this language.

Most of the information in this chapter comes from two books by Dr. Jan Pouwer (1955, 2010). Some additional information was gleaned from Todd Harple's (2000) doctoral dissertation.

Effects on the environment

The Kamoro homeland consists of some 300 kilometers of coastline from Etna Bay to the Otakwa River, reaching inland, through mangrove swamps and tropical rain forest, toward the foothills of the central mountains. Settlement sizes and village dispersal depend on the natural resources available. Toward the west, the high mountains reach close to the coast. Here sago fields are lacking, and the staple must be sought to the east. Villages are smaller and further apart. The area acquired a measure of importance when trade with the outside world gave the Kamoro 'far west' its importance thanks to the acquisition of much-wanted trade goods: especially metal tools and cloth, exchanged for birds-of-paradise plumes, '*massoy*' bark and slaves. Toward the east, where the mountains are further from the coast, a larger hinterland that includes extensive sago swamps, allows for more and bigger villages, sometimes with two important settlements on a major river – one inland, and one on or near the coast. Village size in general increased from the northwest to the southeast.

The various authors writing about the Kamoro underline the basic principle of duality (such as east-west, inland-seashore, bride givers and bride takers, male-female, uncles-nephews). These concepts are linked by mutual obligations in reciprocity where this is possible.

A term named *'aopao'* represents this basic glue of social cohesion. Pouwer defines the word as 'counter-service, counter-action, counter-gift, exchange or barter, response, revenge and retaliation. The concept applies most strongly to the people closest to each other, with diminishing influence usually corresponding to geographical distance. This basic reciprocity is usually applied in the positive sense or mutual help, but it can also cover the concept of an 'eye for an eye'. While the environment of the Kamoro is a very rich one (as long as the population numbers are not too high), many aspects of exploiting natural resources are best done in groups, whence the importance of mutual help in return for past assistance.

The word *'aopao'* can be translated as 'reciprocity' or 'mutual obligation'. An example can be the bride takers who have an obligation to the bride givers, such as helping in their work, providing a canoe or taking care of their bride givers' sons in the initiation rituals. On a different scale, it can mean the obligation that Freeport has to the Kamoro whose lands it took for building the lowlands part of its infrastructure. The Kamoro can interpret the concept of *'aopao'* in many ways. It can sometimes be thought of as a failure to provide adequate compensation.

Kamoro villages in Pouwer's time (and still today) hold populations ranging from 150 to some 600. This contrasts with the larger Asmat settlements that can sometimes reach over 2,000. Village size usually depends on the concentration of nearby sago stands. The largest Kamoro settlements are located midway along rivers east of Kokonau due to optimal balance in available natural resources, between tidal and freshwater swamps.

The *'peraeko'*

The term *'peraeko'* covers a group of Kamoro who are the matrilineal descendants of a specific woman. This applies in particular to the speaker when designating the matrilineal kin emphasis. The term, according to Pouwer, literally means 'one shared vagina'. The word encompasses a named female ancestor's children and grandchildren. The *'peraeko'* itself is usually named after the common female ancestor. Females form the core of the *'peraeko'*, although males are included as well. Harple mentions a direct correlation between the matri-focus of the *'peraeko'* and the traditional residence patterns, land tenure and workgroups. Wild sago groves, the Kamoro's principal dietary source of carbohydrates, are collectively owned by specific '*peraeko*'. The '*peraeko*' members often work together in sago production and fishing parties. They usually live in the same area of a village.

The '*peraeko*' concept is a difficult one for outsiders who are used to exclusive male dominance in patriarchies. Thus, to repeat the meaning of this grouping in slightly different words, the '*peraeko*' extends along one or more generations in a horizontal fashion in that the combined females, as well as the males of a generation, are joined in a particular group by having a common female grandmother. The '*peraeko*' also includes three of these horizontal layers or three generations. The name of the group usually is the same as the ancestral grandmother. In the fourth descending generation, the focal term of reference shifts the name to another woman. While the matrilineal basis is paramount, the group's representative to the outside world is an older brother.

The '*taparu*'

The word '*taparu*' comes from the word '*tapare*', meaning land or territory, with a connotation of a physical area where the group lives. The '*taparu*' determines the rights of land ownership, especially for the sago stands. Quite frequently names of '*taparu*' are identical with or derived from the names of the territories they live on (or once lived on). Other '*taparu*' names refer to human beings, animals, birds, plants or natural phenomena featured in tales and narratives. These however, are not considered ancestors but may be associated with a particular '*taparu*' or set of '*taparu*' in terms of mythical powers or ritual functions ascribed to members of a '*taparu*'.

The '*taparu*' sometimes defined as clan (although Pouwer insists the two terms are not the same) combines a number of matrilineal '*peraeko*'. While the '*peraeko*', with a relatively small number of constituent units, tends to be exogamous (marrying outside the particular '*peraeko*'), the '*taparu*' is often large enough and has enough kinship distance to provide allowable marriage partners to its members. This is especially true when the '*peraeko*' forming the '*taparu*' are unrelated to each other. Within marriage arrangements, the Kamoro recognize and practice a clear distinction between superior bride givers and inferior bride receivers, combined with a preference for matri-local marriage.

The '*peraeko*' groupings (sometimes related or allied, but not necessarily so) that combine to form a '*taparu*' consider themselves closely related, even if the genealogical connections are hazy or hardly known. The concept of kinship is flexible. What matters most is the 'residential override' of who lives (and has lived in the proximity) in the same settlement. Pouwer underlines this by writing that within the larger '*taparu*', such as in the Wania region, the number of constituent '*peraeko*' sets is bigger, and their genealogical relationships are quite removed. During the Kamoro's semi-nomadic existence, it was usual for each '*taparu*' to live together in a thatched, contiguous cubicle-like lean-to hut with shared roofs and woven mat walls but with an individual entrance for each family.

Each '*taparu*' claims and inhabits a particular territory along the main rivers and/or the countless tributaries, with even the smallest having its own name. Formerly, they moved between semi-permanent longhouses and temporary settlements located near fishing and sago grounds. The longhouses were a number of simple lean-to structures, contiguous with only a thin leaf-mat separation between them. Temporary moves between fishing and sago ground still occur today. But, in the permanent settlements there are no longer any longhouses, but individual family units. These were formerly forced on the Kamoro in the early days of colonialism but have now become part of the Kamoro culture. When the Kamoro exploit the natural resources of an area away from their villages, they build modified longhouses, with adjacent family spaces under one roof and sharing sidewalls.

Pouwer defines the word '*otepe*' as secret. A bit more thoroughly, Father Coenen (as quoted by Harple) wrote that this concept referred to power over natural and supernatural events. The '*otepe*' of the various '*peraekos*' is linked to a physical land area, while male-owned '*otepe*', inherited along patrilineal lines (usually father to son), involves many different aspects of Kamoro life. Many more of these secrets are owned by males than by the women, but unlike the '*peraeko*', the male-inherited secrets do not have an overall group name.

According to Harple, the various '*taparu*' (as well as some villages) are so closely associated with their '*otepe*' that they are referred to by their '*otepe*' names. Among many, these include the '*o-we*' (pig people), '*miwi-we*' (spirit people), '*ekaka-we*' (fish people) and '*ku-we*' (canoe people). This last group holds ownership and influence over the kinds of trees suitable for making canoes. Other '*otepe*' cover medical procedures using plants, invoking the supernatural or other techniques. The medicine men's sons inherit specialist

SOCIAL STRUCTURE | 17

cures for different diseases. All these *'otepe'* are passed along the male line, usually from fathers and uncles to sons. This also applies similarly to the right to carve, along with the use of the title *'maramo-we'*.

The village

Due to pressures from the government and the Roman Catholic Church, the Kamoro villages have become quite different than they were in pre-contact days. As we saw above, in the old days, the Kamoro lived in longhouses made up of adjoining cubicles each with its entrance, sharing sidewalls with their immediate neighbors. In the interior, nuclear families were separated from one another by woven-leaf partitions. Today, villages are made up of individual nuclear family dwellings, but often other relations live with the family for short or long periods of time.

Pouwer's early 1950s census of some 8,500 Kamoro found a total of 160 *'taparu'*. These units were grouped into 50 villages, called tribes by Pouwer. The *'taparu'* varied considerably in size. Some were so small that three died out during Pouwer's two years of fieldwork. The settlements only held the communal longhouses. There were no men's or bachelors' houses as with the Asmat where a high degree of male solidarity resulted from the essential cooperation in intensive, continuous warfare.

About half of the Kamoro settlements in the 1950s were made up of two *'taparu'*. Each *'taparu'* had its few elders acting as leaders, but not vested with any sort of absolute power. These positions were non-hereditary and carried few if any privileges. The village that resulted from the union of two or more *'taparu'* only had what Pouwer called 'diffuse' leadership. The concepts of *'kepala desa'* (village chief) and *'kepala suku'* (leader of customs or traditions) are recently introduced concepts. The Kamoro social organization did not favor a single political figurehead as an overall settlement leader. Numerous functionaries and ritual specialists held the 'diffuse' leadership. During the time I spent with the Kamoro, I was occasionally told about a leader referred to as *'we-aiku'*. Based on personality and generous nature, very few men merited this title, and these men were renowned in many villages.

The *'taparu'* were not divided internally into inter-marrying halves (a concept called moiety). After two or more *'taparu'* united into a settlement, they tended to fit into dualistic up-river and down-river groupings. These larger units provided a measure of security and safety in numbers.

An early European color drawing of Uta, a Kamoro village. It illustrates the long communal building shared by all the inhabitants.

The male-oriented '*otepe*' secrets mentioned above also applied to aspects of the various rituals practiced by the Kamoro. Thus, a settlement was able to perform a number of rituals thanks to including complementary specialists belonging to two or more '*taparu*'.

The various settlements exercised a degree of land ownership. While based on the '*peraeko*' land inheritance ('here lived our mother and mother's mothers), the rights applied more to the resources than to actual possession of the land and fishing waters. Pouwer wrote that the right of the disposal of the '*taparu*' was subordinated to that of the village. The village collectively owned the principal rivers, the beach and the near sea.

As in other traditional societies, bride giver groups are considered superior to bride takers. A balance of sorts is restored by the role given to the '*kaoka-paiti*', the brothers-in-law. As in other matriarchies, a man marries into his wife's social group after marriage, and he owes services to his affinal relatives. The main function of the daughter's or sister's husband is to perform crucial duties in rituals for their nephews.

AT PARIMAU
The headman with his stone club.

A Kamoro headman in a photo taken by C. G. Rawling of the British Ornithological Expedition who also wrote a book about their travails.

EARLY KAMORO CONTACTS WITH THE OUTSIDE WORLD

3

A traditional Kamoro multi-family dwelling. The Dutch government imposed nuclear family dwellings in the 1930s. Photo by A.F.R. Wollaston of the British Ornithological Expedition.

It can be taken for a fact that the Kamoro had contacts with other Papuan groups since they first settled in their current homeland. These contacts probably included warfare, trade, and mutual cultural borrowings. This applies to almost if not all Papuan groups, and indeed it is a worldwide phenomenon: ethnolinguistic entities interact with their neighbors. Then, it is very probable that the Kamoro, at least those living in the western area of their current homeland, had various contacts with the outside world for hundreds of years. (Swadling, 1996)

Just who influenced who is a tantalizing but impossible-to-answer question. For example, were the Kamoro influenced by the Malayo-Polynesian groups in the making of their ancestor figures, the *'wemawe'*? The Austronesian *'korwar'* ancestral figures had a wide diffusion where these groups settled on the north coast and in a few pockets on the southwest. Or did the *'wemawe'* carvings influence the shape of the *'korwars'*? An Austronesian language group, called the Kowiai, is presently located as far away along the coast as Etna Bay, the westernmost area of the Kamoro. Could this group have introduced working metal to the Kamoro? The Kowiai certainly did not introduce their very typical (and superior) canoe construction that featured outriggers and sails.

It is certain that either directly or through intermediary groups, the Kamoro were in contact with the areas to the west and north before documented contacts were first made with the world outside of West New Guinea.

The Kamoro's first contact with the outside world was with traders from eastern Indonesia, perhaps over 1,000 years ago. There are no reliable written records concerning West New Guinea before the arrival of the first Europeans in the Moluccas, with the possible exception of a document called Negarakertagama, dated 1365, from the Majapahit Empire centered in East Java. Before the arrival of Europeans, the western part of the Kamoro area was the south-easternmost extremity of a commercial network that connected the southwest coast of New Guinea with Eastern Indonesia. The westernmost extension of this trade network stopped at Lakahia Island, at the entrance to Etna Bay. (Ellen, 1986)

The main items traded by the (westernmost) Kamoro were bird-of-paradise plumes, slaves and the bark of the *'massoy'* tree. The oil from the bark is used in folk medicines and such as various Javanese *'jamu'* (herbs), cosmetics, perfumes, food flavoring and dye-fixing as in the batik industry. The Kamoro probably sold slaves, or some were simply captured by the traders from the west, based in Seram Island and some small islands to the southeast of Seram. The traders brought metal items and clothing to the western edge of the Kamoro area.

It is most likely that the first direct Kamoro trade contacts took place with a network based on several small islands (Seram Laut) off the southeast coast of Seram. (Swadling, 1996) Later, a few of these Seram traders might have settled among the Kamoro.

Seram Laut trading was based on an arrangement called 'sosolot'. This involved a group maintaining a monopoly over certain bays and anchorages. This monopoly was taken by the first group to arrive there and defended to death against other traders. The Seram Laut men who established these trade networks sometimes married Papuan women, usually converting them to Islam. The 'sosolot' system remained effective until around 1900. At that time, Kaimana was the largest trading center that included the eastern Kamoro area. After 1900, Chinese traders seeking bird-of-paradise plumes replaced the Seram Laut 'sosolot' system and became the Kamoro groups' principal trading partners.

First contacts with Europeans

Starting in the early 1500s, the Portuguese, Spaniards, English and Dutch sailed to the Moluccas to seek highly valued spices: cloves, nutmeg and mace. We have just one fascinating source about the south coast of West New Guinea from the early part of this period. In the 1606 journal of Capt. Diego de Prado y Tovar, we have a reference to iron working in Triton Bay, just west of the Kamoro area. Using bellows to heat imported metal, smiths made adzes and harpoons. (Kamma, 1973)

A Kamoro legend tells of a cultural hero named Tamatu who traveled west and taught the Papuans at Triton Bay how to forge iron. This exploit is highly unlikely but fits in with the pattern of the Kamoro that gives them credit for originating items and techniques that they received from the outside world. An example of this mentality is the English who first introduced corn (maize) in East Africa in the mid-19th century. This crop rapidly became a staple, and its origins were integrated into legends and myths, to the point that many in this area firmly believe that corn is their own ancestral crop.

In 1606 the VOC acquired special rights from the Sultan of Tidore to obtain slaves and other goods from the West New Guinea mainland, and nearby islands. By the 1620s, Dutch officials based in the Aru Islands formally recognized the authority of the local 'orang kaya' (leading merchants) along the coast of West New Guinea, in exchange for exclusive trade privileges. (Ellen, 1986) However, the Dutch were unable to break the trade monopoly held by the Muslim traders from Seram, then based on Namatote Island, located between present-day Kaimana and Triton Bay. These Muslim traders dealt in slaves, birds-of-paradise, and 'massoy' bark, in exchange mostly for metal tools and cloth. The western Kamoro must have received some of these goods, as 'massoy' trees grow as far east as the Omba River.

During early pre-colonial times, the peninsula just south of Bintuni Bay, where Fakfak is located, was called Onin, while the area between Arguni Bay and Etna Bay was referred to as Kowiai. The area covered by this term was gradually extended to the east, well into Kamoro lands, as far as the village of Uta. Today, the term Kowiai refers to a particular language group that covers only some of the geographical area.

In 1623 the VOC (the Dutch East India Company) government in Ambon sent captain Jan Carstensz to investigate the trade possibilities off the coast of southwest West New Guinea. Carstensz glimpsed a snow-capped mountain in the interior as he sailed past the Kamoro coast. For several centuries this peak, the highest in New Guinea (4,884m.), was known as Carstensz Toppen (Peak). At the settlement of Mupuruka, the Kamoro, for reasons unknown, killed ten of his men. Perhaps, previous visitors or traders had killed some Kamoro? Or, had the Dutch cut down coconut trees without permission? (Muller, n.d.)

On subsequent expeditions to the southwest Papuan coast, the Dutch lost more men until they finally gave up their attempts at trade, leaving commerce in the hands of the Muslim traders from Seram. By 1670, Namatote had become an important trade center, led by a raja that appointed agents on the islands of Aiduma and Lakahia. From Lakahia, outside influence and trade spread to the western Kamoro area. Titles were freely given out to Kamoro trade partners. (Ellen, 1986)

Dutch activity along the Kamoro coast resumed in the 1800s. The colonial power was afraid that the British (or perhaps the French or the Germans) would establish a foothold in West New Guinea to claim a part of the territory. Fort Du Bus was built in 1828 at Lobo, in the inner reaches of Triton Bay. But it lasted only eight years before diseases and the hostility of local Papuans forced its evacuation.

A large structure built for an initiation ritual. Today the Kamoro build similar ones for the same purpose. Photo by C. G. Rawling of the British Ornithological Expedition who also wrote a book about their travails.

A DANCING HALL.
Erected at the mouth of the Mimika River.

In the same year as the building of Fort Du Bos, two Dutch ships, the Triton and the Iris, landed some men at Utanata (probably at or near present-day Uta). Two of these men provided the first written accounts of Kamoro society: a naval officer and the zoologist S. Muller. In their accounts, we find the first documented Kamoro names: those of two chiefs, one called Abrauw-Mimiti and the other, Makaai. (Muller, 1857). S. Muller remarked on the frenzied trade with the Kamoro at Uta where the natives competed with each other and were keen to obtain the western goods quickly. The Kamoro were mostly after cloth, knives, empty bottles and iron tools. They were not very interested in mirrors or copper rings.

A Dutch report states that also in the same year, 1828, there was a colony of traders from Seram at Abrauw (?) or Uta or Kipia.

Where the Kamoro had extensive contacts with traders from Seram, they dressed in Malay fashion and used titles such as '*kapitan*', '*raja*' and '*hakim*' (judge). They obtained textiles, beads and metal gongs in exchange for '*massoy*', birds-of-paradise and slaves. (Earl, 1837).

Events since the 1850s

In 1858, the Dutch ship Etna visited Lakahia and Etna Bay, later named after this ship. By the middle of the 1800s, with Dutch backing, the trade monopolies of the Seram traders became seriously threatened by the Sultan of Tidore. He sent out '*hongi*' expeditions, large canoes filled with armed men to obtain forced tribute. While most of these raids were aimed at Papua's north coast, the Sultan also directed and sent raiding parties as far as Lakahia Island. Letters of appointment were given to the rajas of Namatote and Aiduma, binding them to Tidore, thus in competition with the Seram traders. (Miklouho-Maclay 1982)

In 1876, the Dutch steamship Soerabaja visited Etna Bay, estimating a total of some 300 people living in four villages. By 1900 the population had declined to about 100. This was partially due to a devastating raid by inland Papuans from Yamur Lake and the upper Omba River. Later, the population there was further reduced by disease (influenza) and alcohol abuse.

When the Russian explorer, Miklouho-Maclay visited Lakahia Island in 1874, he reported on a '*hongi*' raid, led by Prince Ali of Tidore that had taken place some 25 years previously. All the huts and coconut trees were destroyed and about one hundred Papuans were enslaved. The rest of the

This accurate map was drawn by the British Ornithological Union Expedition showing that they did not reach their objective in the central mountain range.

terrified inhabitants fled to settle on the mainland. (Miklouho-Maclay 1982) Probably as a result of this raid, the Papuan inhabitants of the coast killed several dozen Muslim merchants and their crews. The Russian was told that traders avoided much of the southwest Papuan coast to the west of Lakahia as they were usually assaulted, and their boats plundered. Many of the local Papuans lived in fear as well, seldom establishing permanent villages. Further to the east of Etna Bay, conditions were more peaceful. Traders from Seram made yearly visits to the Kamoro village of Uta. In 1850, the Raja of Namatote appointed a raja at the village of Kipia to facilitate trade there. He controlled a district called Tarja that included the villages of Porauka in the west to Uta and Mupuruka in the east.

The Roman Catholic Church made an attempt in 1896 to bring Christianity to the Kamoro. Father C. le Coq d'Armandville visited the area, but he probably drowned or perhaps was killed. Then in 1910, a mission from the Kei Islands visited Kamoro-land but due to the difficulties presented by nature such as sandbank barriers, currents, problems in anchoring and landing, along with none-too-friendly Kamoro, it was decided that this was neither the time nor the place to begin missionary effort in this part of West New Guinea.

Around 1900 the fearsome Naowa of Kipia, leader of the west Mimikan federation of the groups from Kipia, Porauka, Akar, Mapar and Wumuka, led raids to the east, reaching the Mimika River. This raja, appointed by the Islamic-trade raja of Namatote, also raided westward-traveling folks from Central and East Mimika who were in search of textiles, ironware and ornaments. Many men and women and children were also captured and sold as slaves. Naowa long remained in the popular imagination, acquiring some mythical features.

About this time, groups from Wania and Kamoro Rivers united with groups of the Koperapoka River and waged war against the nearby and powerful Tipuka originating from further east. Land rights were perhaps the basic reason for this war, but it was triggered by accusations that the Timika folks had carelessly handled sacred masks so that women could see them. Tipuka lost the war, and refugees as well as children of prisoners of war spread out over Central and West Mimika as far as Etna Bay. (Offenberg, 2002)

Life along the southwest coast of West New Guinea became relatively peaceful after the establishment of a Dutch post at Fakfak in 1898. Muslim traders lost most of their influence. Chinese and Indonesian bird-of-paradise hunters penetrated Kamoro lands, bringing metal tools and red cloth as trade items for payment of services. Chinese traders came mostly for birds-of-paradise, but also *'dammar'*, *'massoy'* and sago, in exchange for axes, machetes, tobacco and betel nuts. They also brought in Chinese dishes and gongs that became important bride wealth items.

Replicated below is a short history of the Dutch exploration of the Kamoro area, based on the UABS Report #7.

During the first decade of the 20th century, the Dutch government embarked on a concerted attempt to explore and map the south coast of Dutch New Guinea. In 1902, Dumas surveyed river entrances along the Mimika coast as far as Newerip (Pisang Bay/Aikwa River), visiting Wakatimi (Mimika) village. Kroesen and de Jongen ascended both the Mimika and Setakwa Rivers in the steam sloop Van Doorn in 1903, and then from 1904 to 1905 the Royal Netherlands Geographical Society's 'Southwest New Guinea' (ZWNG) Expedition conducted an intensive series of surveys along the Mimika coast.

This was followed by a second major survey, the Dutch Military Expedition of 1907–15, led by A.J. Gooszen, which mapped almost every major river on the Mimika coast to its navigable limits. In the course of the Military Expedition, Hellwig ascended the Mimika River (1907), Captain Koch explored the Omba River (1910); van der Ploeg visited Etna Bay (1910); and de Jong and Dumas rowed up the Mimika River as far as Wakatimi. In 1910, a survey that reached deepest into the Mimika hinterland, Lieutenants van der Bie, Dumas and Postema, accompanied by the English naturalist Meek, ascended the Utakwa and Setakwa rivers to a point only 30 km from the snowline. Two years later, Captain Weyerman and Lieutenant Chaillet explored the Akimuga, Ipukwa, Otakwa and Setakwa rivers, and Lieutenant Feuilletau de Bruyn explored the Otakwa river area. In 1913, Lieutenant Ilgen systematically surveyed each of the rivers between the Otakwa and Kamoera Rivers and visited Lakahia with Captain Helb. Given the length of time that these various survey expeditions spent on the Mimika coast, surprisingly little was documented of Kamoro society during these surveys.

This expedition, which included Lieutenant A. van de Water and a Dutch military escort, followed the Utakwa River using Sempan rowers; they noted the cultural and linguistic differences between Sempan and Kamoro, particularly when Kamoro friends from Nimé rowed up the Utakwa River to greet the expedition. No settlements were seen on the Utakwa River itself, but the adjacent Inauga and Omauga (Omawita) rivers were certainly occupied by the ancestors of the current populations of these settlements.

While these expeditions produced little information about the Kamoro, this was soon rectified. The next group of scientists, under the auspices of the British Ornithological Union, provides us with a plethora of facts about the Kamoro, dating from now over a century ago.

For very complete information on trade for art and artefacts by the various Dutch expeditions and early art dealers, see K., 2011, *Collecting Kamoro*.

THE KAMORO 100 YEARS AGO: THE BRITISH ORNITHOLOGICAL UNION EXPEDITION

4

Contemporary Kamoro nuclear family huts. The Kamoro were persuaded to build single-family huts by the Dutch government and the Roman Catholic Church.

Temporary multi-family dwellings called **'kapiri kame'** (house of pandanus leaves) are erected today when seeking food away from the villages.

The first reliable account of the Kamoro lifestyle comes from the British Ornithological Union's (BOU) expedition that was based at Wakatimi Village, near present-day Kokonau, for 15-months from 1911 to 1912. The main purpose of the expedition was to reach the glaciers and the peak of Puncak Jaya (Carstensz Peak, Nemangkawi Ninggok). After many months of heart-breaking attempts, and a number of deaths, the expedition did not even come close to its goal. However, success was claimed in that the team discovered a group of pygmies who lived in the foothills just north of the Kamoro area. These Papuans, either of the Me or Moni language group, were not really pygmies, nor were the British the first to discover short mountain Papuans. A previous Dutch expedition had already contacted what they called the 'Goliath Pygmies'. (Goliath referred to the name of a nearby mountain, *not* to the size of the pygmies.) The BOU members had close contact with the Kamoro for the duration of the expedition. The members of the expedition, Wollaston and Rawling, each wrote a book about their experiences where we can find a wealth of information about the traditional life of the Kamoro before the group was brought under the influence and control of the Dutch government and the Roman Catholic Church.

As no one in the BOU spoke the Kamoro language, and at the time no Kamoro spoke Malay/Indonesian, the expedition accounts can only provide us with information mostly on the material culture of the Kamoro. It was only after a few outsiders (two priests and an anthropologist) learned the language that information became available on their social structure, myths and supernatural beliefs.

However, the two British authors, Wollaston and Rawling, give us a relatively complete glimpse of what they could see during the time they spent in close contact with the Kamoro. Sometimes these two accounts are somewhat different about the same subject. Many aspects of this lifestyle are forgotten today. (Wollaston, 1912) (Rawling 1913)

Canoes

Take canoes for instance. Wollaston wrote that the canoes he saw had 'a narrow margin of carving at intervals along the sides... Occasionally they attach to the bow of the canoe, one on either side and one in the middle, three longboards carved in a sort of fretwork manner and painted red and white. These project about four feet in front of the bow and give it the appearance of a bird's beak. ... The natives take great care with their boats; outside charred with fire to kill the [boring] worms... the most common tree used for canoes is the *Octomeles muluccana*. The paddles have wide blades, often beautifully carved.' Rawling adds that the elaborate fretwork decorations were fixed upright on the canoe bows during festive occasions.

The BOU was fortunate in that the Kamoro of Wakatimi were willing to sell their canoes, as the expedition had no other way of making their way upstream and inland. The men were 'all too anxious to trade their canoes, at first for a handkerchief or a small knife, later for two axes'. These canoes were up to 18 meters long and were burned on the outside to prevent what Rawling wrongly calls 'water insects', in reality, a boring marine mollusk of the genus *Toredo*, wood and ship worms.

Very few canoes show any carving today. The canoes used in the east, made for river and estuary travel, end in a wide, flat forward prow. These are called '*ku*'. To the west, where the canoes often are taken out to sea, the prow comes to a high point to cut through the waves. These are called '*torpa*'. The canoes in the east are usually paddled standing up, with men, women and children all displaying, as Wollaston put it, 'wonderful feats of balancing'. '*Torpa*'-style canoes are paddled from a sitting position.

A century ago, the Kamoro of Parimau Village had but one small piece of iron 'the size of a chisel, used for their canoes and paddles, for which they paid the enormous price of three dogs to the people of Wakatimi Village'. Today, chainsaws are sometimes used to help fell a tree for a canoe or a drum, while steel axes and various carpenter tools are in de rigueur for the shaping and hollowing out to finish off.

Dwellings and settlements

The BOU's main base was located some five kilometers from the sea, across the Mimika River from the Kamoro village called Wakatimi. It was further inland than the contemporary four-village complex of Kokonau, a short distance north of where the Kapare River joins the Mimika. Wollaston describes Wakatimi Village as a single street some 200 meters long, lined on one side by some 60 contiguous huts (Rawling wrote 'about 150 huts built of pandanus and palm leaves' as are today's thatched temporary huts) with no dividing walls between them. Rawling stated that the village was 'one long room, with new arrivals building onto the ends. These extensions turned the village into one endless habitation, broken by their respective doorways. Each family had an interior partition on each side of its space. The floors were sand brought from the seashore. The dwelling's top covering was a low, sloping thatch roof coming up from the ground at the back to the front, about 1.5 m high. The front could be closed off with interwoven strips of leaves. Skulls and bones dangled from the roof. Cylindrical wood pillows were the only 'furniture'. These were some 10 cm wide, about 70 cm long and 'so decorated with carvings as not to leave one square inch of smooth surface for the neck'.

While some Kamoro villages have retained their names, many have shifted location. The BOU made a map with village names that existed then. The BOU description of some villages varies, with quick and superficial observations: some positive and some negative. Rawling wrote that the Atuka River is deeper than most others and hosts the 'great straggling village of Atuka on the right bank, just below a great bend; the huts lie in an unbroken line for close to 1500 meters, except for two great dancing halls'. To Rawling, Atuka was the 'largest and cleanest village, with a pleasant background of coco-nut, breadfruit trees and with tobacco plantations beyond'. His opinion of Kamura Village is quite negative: 'the majority of women are in a complete state of nudity [as are the men]. Here Rawling notes about 250 huts and a population of 1000 to 1500. He experienced a 'tense stand off' and calls this group 'avaricious and degraded.... not exactly hostile but bent on robbing', but who also very much wanted to trade.

The semi-nomadic lifestyle of the Kamoro is shown graphically when Wollaston wrote that 'there are sometimes 1000 persons living there [Wakatimi], and sometimes not a single soul'. The village owned a fine grove of coconut palms. The coconuts were exchanged for tobacco and bananas and sweet potatoes with the inhabitants of Obata (or Obota) Village, located close by on the Kapare River. At the time, Nime Village was the most important one in the area.

Clothing

Most of the men of Parimau Village wore a narrow, short strip of bark cloth or a bamboo penis sheath that was always carved with ornamental

A memorial to Father Le Coq d'Armandville, the Roman Catholic priest who attempted but failed to introduce his faith to the Kamoro. He was either killed by the Kamoro or drowned off the coast of the Arafura Sea.

designs. Some of them wore a large white shell, up to 15 cm in diameter. The foreskin of the penis was pulled upward and placed under the lower margin of the shell. This was the style of the Marind men in the Merauke area. Today the Kamoro only remember their ancestors wearing bark cloth prior to the arrival of modern clothing. They state that only the Sempan ethnic group, living to the east of them, wore the decorated bamboo penis sheaths. Father Zegwaard, who learned to speak the Kamoro language, wrote that the bamboo penis sheath was more common inland while the use of the shell was more frequent on the coast. (Zegwaard, 1995)

The women wore bark cloth. Widows' headpieces, projecting forward, were made of 'ingeniously plaited fiber'. Children were strapped on with bark cloth. Sharp fish bones needles and fiber thread were used to sew the pieces of bark cloth very neatly together. Wollaston noticed that the inhabitants of Atuka and Kamura villages wore nothing at all, 'both men and women go completely naked'. The Asmat men wore no clothing either, up to the 1950s. The Kamoro at Wakatimi were taller than the average European, and to Rawling, the men with 'splendidly developed muscles, physically almost perfect.... the upriver Kamoro are similar in build but more pleasing appearance and superior in intellect to the coastal tribes'.

Wollaston points out that many of the men filed or chipped their upper incisor teeth to a point. The septum of the nose was pierced in all young men. Rawling wrote that this was part of the boys' initiation at the age of 10 or 12. A piece of hornbill beak or curved boar's tusk was inserted in the resulting hole. Tattooing was not practiced, but fire-induced scarring resulted in a 'cross surrounded by a circle on the right buttock; on the left one, a cross was burned, about 5 cm. square'. Rawling calls these 'tribal markings on the buttocks, shaped like a diamond, with lines radiating from the corners'. Faces were sometimes 'painted bright red with a type of clay, or smeared with a mixture of fat and charcoal, or whitened with sago powder'.

Rituals and Art

During their long stay in the Kamoro area, the Europeans saw some rituals and examples of art. But they were unable to find out any meanings due to the lack of a common language. Nevertheless, even the superficial descriptions are valuable as many aspects of the traditional religious life were abandoned before they could be better described. And, while some aspects remain the same, others are modified. An example of this comes from Rawling who wrote that 'women can't sing but dance only, men don't dance'.

Wollaston describes various group activities, some of which were filmed by the BOU: '.... about 150 men with faces painted and spears decorated with feathers formed up on three sides of the square, one end of which was occupied by a band of drums. A slow advance on the village then commenced, the men shouting in chorus and the women dancing on the outskirts. The centre of the square was occupied by a single individual, who, following each other in quick succession, gave a warlike display, finally shooting arrows far over the treetops. ... Two boars, on each of which a man sat astride, were now hoisted up and carried to the altar, on which the animals were tightly lashed... clubbed to death; women cut the carcasses free and threw themselves on the dead bodies, wailing loudly and plastering themselves with wet mud in ecstasies of grief... Just previous, a three-year old child, painted red and crying loudly, had been roughly seized and dragged toward the dais: ears pierced. ... Women and girls - many of them quite pretty - chasing the men up to the riverside and into the water. This is one of the few ceremonies when the women are allowed to beat the men, the latter not permitted to retaliate. The damsels finally became so bold they stormed the [BOU] camp.'

The art of the Kamoro also drew their attention: 'They make curiously carved effigies, but these are not idols; they treat them with contempt and point to them with laughter; These images are ingenious and skillfully carved out of wood and they represent a human figure always grotesque and sometimes grossly indecent. They vary in size from a few inches to 12 or 14 feet, and when not neglected they are ornamented with red and white paint.' Sharpened shells were used for carving, as very little metal was available.

At Nime Village, the expedition members saw a very elaborate 'dancing house; the ridge pole at either end had a very lifelike representation of the head of a crocodile, painted red...six smaller poles with grotesquely carved representations of fish and reptiles and hideous human heads... round the walls on all sides was a strip of carved and painted wood, and exactly in the middle of the hall, fixed to the floor and the roof were two posts about one meter apart and tied between them, at about half the height of a man, was an elaborately carved and painted board about twelve inches wide. In the middle of this board was carved the eye... a familiar feature in ornamental carving... on canoes and drums... each participant touched the eye and shouted together.'

Rawling wrote of the same event, describing a 'dancing floor built on piles, three meters above ground, in a 220 by 80-meter square area. Around the lower part of the interior walls, about a meter from the floor, the Kamoro had placed 'a plank of wood, on which were carved representations of the human eye at intervals of about 60 cm..... in the center, another short plank was covered with more carved human eyes.... the dance was based on these carvings... the women danced back and forth and when approaching sufficiently close, poked at the eyes with their fingers, accompanying this action with a loud shout.'

Fishing and weapons

A century ago, as today, fishing was a mainstay of the Kamoro lifestyle. Fish provides the main source of protein. With no method of preservation, fishing was a daily occupation. Once, in a most unusual clear-water area (all waters are usually filled with suspended particles), Rawling saw fish of 'every imaginable color and shape seemed to have a representative.... round fish, square fish, fish as flat as a piece of paper and long and thin as pencils, spiky fish and smooth fish.... all in a hundred vivid hues and brilliant spots, stripes and blotches.'

While today most fish are caught in large nets, there is no mention of this method in the BOU books. Then and now, branches of estuaries were blocked off with a weir, a trelliswork or curtain of sticks or strips of bamboo. This curtain was pulled across the narrow waterway at high tide. As the water level dropped with the outgoing tide, the fish that had been feeding upstream were trapped behind the weir and could easily be caught by hand.

There were only a few native hooks used in fishing. These hooks were of various patterns, made from shells, fishbones or bamboo, some plain, some barbed. The metal fishhooks brought in by the outsiders were highly appreciated by the Kamoro. By one account, larger fish were caught using hook and line or a spear in shallow waters. In another account, in deeper waters, spears and arrows were used, along with harpoons with detachable heads. Along with various species of larger fish, dugongs and dolphins were also hunted with harpoons. There is no mention of hunting crocodiles practiced today with detachable head harpoons. The Kamoro charred their fish and so could keep them for a few days. Rawling comments that 'if they learned to smoke them, they would never go hungry'.

The Japanese advanced on the south coast of West New Guinea as far as the Kamoro village of Kekwa. A memorial in that village was built by the Japanese for the souls of their fellow soldiers who died there.

The expedition traded for fish and 'delicious prawns, 15 to 20 cm. long from the estuary'. The Kamoro also bartered coconuts, cassowaries, artifacts and all sorts of objects, including the 'skulls of the ancestors' for all types of European goods, including colored beads, red cloth, knives of various sizes and axes. 'Red cloth was the most sought after.... and the natives never tire of using of steel axes' obviously superior to their stone tools. The Kamoro also supplied all the thatching required for the expeditions of many buildings.

The Kamoro bows were described as made of pandanus wood, ornamented with cassowary claws or tufts of feathers, shells or crab claws. Arrows were sometimes tipped with a sharp cassowary claw or a stingray spine. There were three kinds of hunting spears. One was quite heavy with a fire-hardened tip, while a second type was lighter and tipped with a sharpened bone tip. The third kind of spear, made of a softwood, was finely pointed and 'with a wide blade carved in some sort of open-work fashion.' (Spears have mostly gone out of fashion today except to hunt wild pigs.) The young boys played at fighting battles with miniature bows and reed stems used as arrows and spears.

Disposal of the dead

The ease with which the Kamoro were willing to trade their ancestors' skulls surprised the Europeans, especially after they had seen elaborate funerary rites. They described the most common practice as burial in a shallow grave, with the body wrapped in mats and laid down flat. In more elaborate funerals, perhaps for more important men, the body was placed on a platform some 1.5m high. Another method was to wrap the body in mats and place it in a crude type of coffin made from an old, broken canoe. This coffin was held above ground by a trestle of crossed sticks until the body decomposed. The body was turned over daily. In some instances, painted and decorated posts were erected at the head and feet of the grave. After the body decomposed, the skulls were preserved in the family's house. But no special affection was shown, or power attributed to the skulls, as they were easy to acquire in trade by the visitors.

Japanese troops built a landing strip for fighter aircraft between Kekwa and Timika Pantai Villages. It was used for a short time by Freeport when the company began a drilling program at the future Ertsberg mine site.

Expedition problems and final opinions

The relations with the Kamoro and the BOU did not start out on a good footing. Rawling wrote about 'the shooting of two savages at Wakatimi in the early days of the expedition, while justifiable, almost led to hostilities'. One wonders how the shooting of two men would *not* have led to hostilities. The BOU had its own carriers, many of them unfit for the tasks they were told to perform. The expedition was made up of about 400 men of several races, of which 12 per cent died. This included a European naturalist who drowned after getting lost in the mangrove swamp. The Kamoro who found his body smeared themselves with mud as their traditional sign of mourning. Of the 400 original members, only 11 lasted the full 15 months with the BOU: four Europeans, four Nepalese soldiers, two military men, and one convict. The rest had to be evacuated due to illness or injury. They were soon replaced.

At one point during the expedition, Wollaston wrote that 'An unprejudiced observer looking upon us from the outside in the evening might well wonder what kind of lunatics we were to come to New Guinea. ... Rains, floods, sickness among coolies and consequent inaction.... there were leeches in my eyes, in my mouth and one was captured as it was about to enter one nostril'.

The relations with the Kamoro were good enough that they did provide some service by paddling canoes from the Wakatimi toward the base to the BOU's upriver camp at Parimau but would only travel some 15 kilometers from home. And most would not work as carriers on land, nor could they be induced to do any manual labor. However, the BOU was able to convince some of them to work carrying food supplies to an inland base camp. Kamoro labor also was partially used for six months in the clearing of a six-hectare tract of land. The expedition surveyors needed this clear space to view the mountains cut off by vegetation, as well as to obtain clear lines of sight for their map work.

Parimau, a Kamoro village located at the end of the navigable portion of the Mimika River held 25 huts. At the village, the BOU was given a tumultuous welcome where the inhabitants 'smeared their bodies with mud and the shed copious tears.' Parimau was located 34 kilometers in a direct line from the coast and 60 kilometers and five to seven days from Wakatimi by the winding river. Rawling concluded that the inhabitants of Wakatimi and Parimau were of the same tribe as both groups showed similar 'tattoos' on their buttocks. The habits of the groups were also similar.

The BOU had many problems with the Kamoro of Wakatimi due to their unwillingness to work, preferring to spend their leisure time under sugar palms getting drunk. Wollaston called them a 'gang of drunkards' and blamed their drinking for being 'entirely responsible for any hostility'. The village was 'in perpetual strife and drunken brawls'. Rawling wrote that drinking often ended up with 'wife beatings, house burnings or some such attractive amusement'. To minimize the temptations, the BOU team cut down all the sugar palms in the vicinity.

Drunk or not, the men tested each other's ability to withstand pain. Using their war clubs, made of coral, limestone or sandstone, they would hit each other on the back, with no flinching allowed. This went on until one of the two opponents had enough. No blows were allowed to the head.

The overall opinion of the expedition about the Kamoro was relatively positive, despite the problems it encountered. While the Kamoro lived a relatively easy life, diseases were common: malarial fevers, boils, pneumonia, elephantiasis, and skin diseases. Syphilis was 'exceedingly prevalent, probably brought by Chinese and Malay traders'. One author mentions that the Kamoro had 'no knowledge of medicinal plants' a statement that we know was completely false. Of course, the level of material culture was a simple one, with no metal or pottery and only the 'rudest of ornaments'. However, 'in spite of such drawbacks, the Papuans of Mimika are not such a miserable people'. True enough, but another opinion has proved completely false. Rawling wrote that this was 'a land whose past is hidden in the mists of time and one without a future, since it can never be occupied by civilized settlers'. Of course, he could not foresee the arrival of the Dutch government, the Roman Catholic Church, and, least of all, the near-incredible development of the Kamoro area that followed the opening of the huge Freeport mine in the mountains.

Enthusiastic participants arrive at the yearly Kamoro festival. Freeport sponsored this festival from 1998 to 2005.

THE DUTCH GOVERNMENT, THE ROMAN CATHOLIC MISSION AND WWII: DRASTIC CHANGES

5

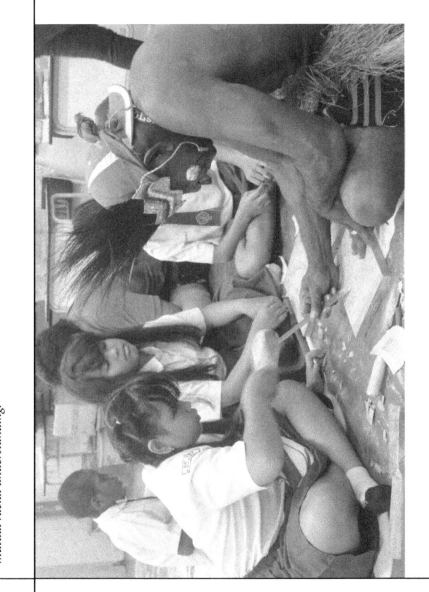

A Kamoro teaches carving to children at a government school as part of an outreach program for mutual racial understanding.

The government post, opened by the Dutch in Kokonau in 1926, brought about the greatest changes to the Kamoro lifestyle. It was established to control the bird-of-paradise plume trade by Chinese buyers. It was first founded at the side of Wakatimi Village (the site of the BOU base) but soon moved to Kokonau.

The following year, the Roman Catholic Church followed from its headquarters in the Kei archipelago. The Catholics had a measure of success in starting a mission near Fakfak where many Papuan Muslims lived, descendants of Muslim traders that had married local women. They were less successful to the south, where Father Le Coq d'Armandville started to explore the Kamoro area before drowning (or perhaps being killed) in 1896. Then in 1910, Father Niejens of the Missionaries of the Sacred Heart (MSC) traveled to the Kamoro homeland to check out the possibilities of establishing a mission outpost there. Unfortunately, on landing in a village on the Mimika River, he witnessed a nose-piercing coming-of-age ritual. He saw women in a frenzy licking up the blood from the initiates' ears and then to top it off, he was horrified by a usual end of ritual battle between the sexes where he found the women behaving like 'female devils'. This was too much for his sensibilities and advised that any mission activities should be postponed. But, both the Dutch government and the Catholic mission wanted to stem the spread of the Muslim faith from Kaimana to the Kamoro area.

So, the government post established in Kokonau also hosted the area's seat of the Roman Catholic mission in 1927. Father Kowatzki was the first priest posted there. In 1930 he was joined by Father (later Bishop) Tillemans, a priest who trekked extensively and explored the area. It was shortly after Father Tillemans' arrival that the first mass baptisms took place in 1933. The two priests divided their area of work, with Father Kowatzki based in Kokonau and 13 nearby villages, while Father Tillemans was based in Uta with a parish that included nine villages. Father Drabbe arrived in 1935 and within a year produced a Kamoro dictionary and grammar. Then another priest, Father Akkermans, arrived in the Mimika area. He also studied the Kamoro language.

According to the UABS report, Kokonau was initially not the most important government post. The European District Officer called Bestuur,

Foreign guest visitors observing a canoe ritual during a visit to a remote Kamoro village. This helps to keep alive ancient traditions.

in Dutch, who headed the new Mimika sub-district was stationed on Yaparo Island, off Otakwa Village. Assistant sub-district officers held their posts at Kokonau, Yapero and Uta. Dutch records show that Felix Maturbongs was the Indonesian (non-European) District Officer at Yapero from 1935 to 1937 when a flood destroyed this post. It was subsequently moved to Agats, in the 1950s, the first government post in the Asmat area.

Positive and negative changes brought about by government presence came at a price for the Kamoro. Every adult had to pay taxes, usually in the form of '*dammar*', a valuable tree resin formerly burnt for lighting, and later used in inks, lacquers, oil paints and varnishes. On the other hand, health measures cut childhood deaths from malaria, introduced much-desired western goods, and stopped cold the deadly Asmat raids.

Changes in Kamoro lives

Prior to the arrival of the mission and the Dutch government, the Kamoro led a semi-nomadic lifestyle. Their homes were very simple, low, slanted thatched roofs coming straight from the ground to about a meter at the front, with an opening to the outside that could be closed off. Families lived together in a long row of these simple structures with a leaf wall dividing each family's space. These traditional homes were called '*kapiri kame*'. The word '*kapiri*' means pandanus leaves and '*kame*' means house. Villages were semi-permanent in that the Kamoro frequently moved between the coast where the best fishing was located, to upriver areas inland where the staple sago and other food resources were found. Land rights, owned by different clans, extended along various rivers.

The Kamoro moved periodically to take advantage of their food resources. But they gathered in large groups for various rituals that took place relatively often. Elaborate structures were built for these festivals and carvings were made by men with hereditary rights to do so.

Nomadic people present an almost impossible task for administrators and missions. So, the Kamoro were persuaded or forced to settle in permanent villages. There had been earlier moves toward semi-permanent settlements at river mouths to trade with Chinese merchants. But these moves were entirely voluntary. In the new government-decreed villages, the Kamoro had to build single-family houses, raised off the ground, with walls of '*gaba-gaba*' (the thick central stem of palm fronds) and a thatch roof.

Both the government and the Roman Catholic Church tried to convince the Kamoro of the advantages of a settled existence in permanent villages. Initially, this move was strongly resisted, with force-built villages often deserted as the Kamoro pursued their shifts between ecosystems. Two government programs, starting in 1930, convinced some Kamoro of the advantages of a more sedentary lifestyle. A school was established in the larger villages in the eastern section, along with a medical program dealing with the principal diseases: malaria, tuberculosis, and yaws.

The Kamoro quickly accepted the Roman Catholic faith, superficially at least. Most of the villages were staffed by teachers from the Kei Islands who formed the base of the Roman Catholic Church in its efforts to proselytize the south coast of West New Guinea. These teachers considered themselves superior to the Kamoro, and often treated them badly. This state of affairs was common with other groups living on the south coast where Kei teachers were also brought in by the church.

Initially, the Kamoro were quite keen on having schools. They probably thought that they could enter the world of much-desired material goods through the schools. However, they soon realized that this was not the case, and that schools disrupted family life. Children, who used to travel with their parents when they went to make sago or seek other food resources were not allowed to leave school. Of course, there was a great deal of absenteeism.

By 1930, there were 24 semi-permanent settlements under some degree of government control. In 1932, the Kamoro area held 21 schools, with some 2,100 students taught by 22 teachers. The instruction focused on religion above all, and the need for order, regular attendance, and hygiene. Subjects included the Malay (Indonesian) language, reading, writing and arithmetic. Few children progressed beyond the third grade.

Between 1930 and 1937 a fierce competition took place for Kamoro souls between the Roman Catholic Church and the Protestant Church of the Moluccas. On the ground, this translated into a parallel system of schools and churches in the villages, the Roman Catholic Kei teachers facing Protestant ones from Ambon. It was a wonderful time for the Kamoro who easily became 'rice Christians', following the religion that gave away more food, clothing, tobacco, metal tools or other items. For a while, the civilian administrator and the Indonesian police favored the Protestants, giving them a measure of advantage to make up for their late start. However, the Catholics eventually prevailed, and the Protestants withdrew from most of Kamoro-land due to a lack of sufficient finances. Their triumph was not so much based on any 'superior' theology, but in being able to count on contributions from their fellow Catholics in Holland to provide freely more material goods: clothes, food, metal tools, tobacco. The results made many Kamoro into 'rice Christians'.

The Protestants attempted again after World War II, but without success. Today, all Kamoro follow the Catholic Church. All the Kamoro that is within the boundaries of the Mimika '*kabupaten*' (district). Three villages to the west, Omba, Lakahia and Warifi, in the Kaimana '*kabupaten*', are Protestant, too far from the mission center at Kokonau.

While no one actually forbade the Kamoro from practicing their traditional culture, it was certainly not encouraged by either the priests, the administrators and least of all by the Kei teachers. Government officials, missionaries and teachers deemed the making of carvings and performing rituals a 'waste of time'. Some priests did show a more flexible attitude toward traditional rituals but not the Protestants. In the Etna Bay area, the Protestants even prohibited drumming and singing outside church services. All outsiders, including the government, objected to the nose-piercing part of the initiation ritual, and this practice was largely dropped, partially as a health measure. However, initiations and some other rituals continued. The Kamoro were also strongly discouraged from following their semi-nomadic existence: free spirits are the bane of governments everywhere. Settled populations can be counted, educated, taxed, made to work, controlled. Wandering folks do as they please, a dangerous precedent.

The rich spiritual life of the traditional Kamoro religion was abandoned, in part at least. Following the advice of the Catholic Church, the Dutch government quickly banned the nose-piercing ritual, along with the mock battles between sexes that usually ended a number of rituals. As the Kamoro's large, important rituals took up too much of their energy, the civil officials stopped many of them, allowing some to be performed only if permission was granted first and most of all, if it did not interfere with more 'worthwhile' duties such as making gardens for their Kei teachers, or attending school.

Today, only the boys' initiation ceremony is still regularly followed in many, but far from all the villages, once every five or six years. But to what degrees have the Kamoro assimilated Christianity is an open question. In 1961, Dr. Jan Pouwer, a Dutch anthropologist, wrote that 'Until now and after 36 years of acculturation, they have not accepted a modern attitude towards life nor the essence of Christian faith – although nearly everyone was baptized.'

Freeport built and sponsored a Kamoro carving workshop in the town of Timika for several years. The carved frontage was later dismantled and taken to a museum in The Netherlands.

THE DUTCH GOVERNMENT, THE ROMAN CATHOLIC MISSION AND WWII: DRASTIC CHANGES | 55

But before we condemn the interference of the outside world on the Kamoro, let us remember that their lifespan was in the order of some 30 years, with infant mortality from malaria reaching 50 per cent of live births. (The population of the whole island of New Guinea, now well over seven million, never exceeded one million until the colonial powers brought in western medicines and forced the cessation of tribal warfare.)

Asmat raids

The presence of the government (and its weapons) brought another positive change to the Asmat. Previously, the Kamoro were a 'prey species' subject to frequent well-organized Asmat headhunting raids. The Kamoro had suffered from Asmat small-scale raids for several generations, but these increased in intensity starting in the late 1920s. The increase in material goods among the Kamoro brought on far larger and more deadly Asmat raids, especially their 'hunger for iron'. There are records of three devastating raids, with many Kamoro heads heading east (minus the bodies of their owners) to decorate Asmat houses and appease bloodthirsty spirits there.

Then the Dutch-trained police and modern firearms drastically swung the balance of forces to the advantage of the Kamoro. A small police force, combined with Kamoro warriors from Atuka and the Wania villages defeated and killed a large Asmat war party in May 1931. The Asmat soon understood that brave, aggressive and clever as they might be, they would only lose their own lives if they persisted in raiding the Kamoro villages.

A hydroplane base in Kamoro-land

In 1936, the Netherlands New Guinea Petrol Company set up a hydroplane base for exploration at Etna Bay, and near the mouth of the Ajkwa River, close to the present Freeport portsite of Amamapare. These bases served an extensive drilling program along the Kamoro coast and the interior. Kamoro families from the Tipuka and Wania communities established camps near the company base at the Ajkwa River. Some men found temporary employment in the menial jobs around the company base camp, as well as clearance of vegetation for drilling and survey lines. They were paid in red cloth, tobacco, and other goods, as money was not in use.

Kamoro from nearby villages repeated the same move over 30 years later when Freeport built its port a short distance inland. Many Kamoro still live on Keraka Island, a few hundred meters from Freeport's modern shipping port.

The Ajkwa base served for an intrepid team of three Dutch explorers who with eight Dayak porters made their way up the Ajkwa River, then (almost) all the way inland to New Guinea's highest peak, Nemangkawi Ninggok, better known as Puncak Jaya. The team's route followed aerial surveys, and supplies were also dropped from the air. During the trek, Jean Jacques Dozy, a geologist and member of the team, discovered a huge aboveground ore body that he called Ertsberg (Ore Mountain). Later, this ore body attracted the American mining company that began extracting copper and gold from there, with the first shipment of concentrated ore in December 1972. This company is now Freeport Indonesia.

During one of the aerial surveys, the Dutch pilot Wissel discovered the large inland Paniai Lakes. The small government outpost in the Kamoro village of Uta became the base for the exploration, then for the supplies of the first highlands government post and Christian missions in the highlands, located at Enarotali. Supplies and personnel traveled upriver from Uta with Kamoro paddlers and their canoes, then trekked overland with Me porters to Enarotali.

While Uta served as the base for the highlands, Yapero Island served a similar function for exploring the area to the east. In 1936 a police post was established at Yapero to prevent any Asmat headhunting raids. And just before WWII, it served as a base for exploring Asmat territory. The Asmat was the last major ethnic group to fall under the sway of the Dutch government and the Roman Catholic Church.

World War II

The arrival of Japanese troops in the western part of the Kamoro area took place in 1942. On December 15, 1942, the Japanese landed in Mimika, on the southern coast of West New Guinea. This was carried out with the ships named Hatsukari and Tomozuru. About 270 officers and men succeeded in landing without encountering Allied counterattack. No specific place was mentioned in the Japanese records. The location was probably either the villages of Timika or Kokonau.

We have a version of this even in the book, *Jungle Pimpernel*. (Rhys, 1947) The author mentions that it was just after this Japanese landing that the Allies in Merauke received a message from Uta, transmitted by the Dutch official, Jean de Bruijn. He had led a party down from his base at Enarotali (on Lake Paniai) to the coast after he and Father Tillemans and Indonesian officials had received letters from the Japanese authorities to report to Fakfak with any radio equipment they owned. Father Tillemans, who received this letter as he was on his way to Uta from Enarotali, returned and advised de Bruijn of the Japanese demands. Far from obeying this order, de Bruijn led a patrol down to Uta to gather intelligence. The men under de Bruijn disarmed a Papuan patrol left by the Japanese at Uta. They learned that the day before their arrival, two Japanese destroyers had passed along the coast off Uta, heading east, towards Timika. 'It was obvious that their intention was to land there and establish an air base.'

'De Bruijn radioed a report of this to the authorities at Merauke and a reconnaissance plane was sent over but reported no activity. Two weeks later, however, a Japanese airstrip was under construction.' While gathering information at Uta, de Bruijn also found out through intercepted correspondence, that 'the two destroyers had put in at Timoeka (now Timika Pantai Village) and landed 450 marines there.

The only location of any strategic importance on most of the south coast was this fighter airstrip built between Kekwa and Timika Pantai villages. Eventually, some 800 Japanese soldiers occupied parts of the Kamoro lands. The Japanese pushed out exploratory patrols as far as the Asmat area. The airstrip was bombed several times by Allied forces in 1944. (This airstrip was later upgraded and used briefly by Freeport starting in 1967, until the current landing field near the present town of Timika was completed.) Timika Pantai and Kekwa villages were strafed, as the Japanese troops were concentrated there.

While the Japanese controlled almost all of present-day West New Guinea, the Allied forces (mostly Australian) established an important military base at Merauke and a smaller one inland at Tanah Merah. From this base, the Allies sent river patrols toward the Japanese-controlled Kamoro area. But most of the land between Yapero and the south Asmat area became a no man's land, with neither side willing to commit much energy to controlling this area. The Japanese however, did put in considerable effort to control the Paniai Lakes area. A strong detachment was sent up from Uta, arriving just after all but three foreigners who were evacuated by hydroplane. A Japanese force remained in this highlands area for much of the rest of WWII.

In 1939, well before the Japanese arrived in the Mimika area, the Dutch government official, Felix Maturbongs from the Kei Islands, was the most senior civil servant at the Yapero/Otakwa district. He made some initial patrols into the Asmat territory. He continued his patrols at the time of the arrival of the Japanese, writing letters about the war situation in his area. From the *Asmat Sketchbooks*, we know that the Japanese killed 22 men from Syuru (reason not given). They also executed 20 married men and a bachelor because they had helped Felix Maturbongs smuggle some correspondence out of the Ayam area.

The Allies had some geographical information from Dutch officials about the Merauke/Mappi/Tanah Merah areas, as well as the Kamoro and north Asmat lands. However, there was no knowledge about the long stretch of territory between the Mappi outpost and the Eilanden River estuary. The Dutch had tried and failed twice to find a passage from the Mappi post to the Wildeman River. They were stopped both times by heavy barrier-islands of floating vegetation and debris. D. Thomson of the Australian Army was given the job of finding a way through this 'impenetrable' swamp area, reputedly impassable and to explore the Eilanden River to its estuary. He had to cover some 350 kilometers of unknown territory. It was essential for the Australians to know if the Japanese had infiltrated the country towards Mappi from their known base in the Kamoro area. Thompson also had to find a location for a forward military post toward the Japanese bases in Kamoro-land.

The Asmat were not at all welcoming to Thompson's Australian unit. Early one morning some 200 Asmat attacked the reconnaissance party. This probably took place near the large Asmat village of Atsj. The Australians were overwhelmed, and all suffered serious wounds. 'The natives were armed with steel axes which they wielded with a flourish as the battle axes of old; with great knives and machetes, and their own heavy stone axes and clubs. But due to their great numbers, after the first onslaught, they could not see where to hit. We turned the machine guns on them and on their moored canoes'. Strangely, Thomson mentions no bows, arrows or spears among the Asmat weapons.

Thanks to their Bren guns and presence of mind, the Australians escaped a short distance upstream. They radioed for help and some 40 hours later, a Catalina hydroplane, escorted by Kittyhawk fighters, brought a relief party and picked up the wounded.

The recon mission was successful in that it established and proved the existence of a water connection between the swamps of the Oba and the Eilanden River. And it found a possible site for an Australian outpost relatively close to the established Japanese positions. Sometime later, Capt. C. C. Wolfe established 'Post 6' at this location in the Asmat area.

Wolfe sent Asmat 'spies' ahead of his patrols who prepared friendly receptions for him. Thus, he was able to find out that there were (in December 1943) no Japanese at Yapero, but that two Japanese soldiers lived at Otakwa, two at Inauga, and 20 of them with a large party of some 200 native police at Koperapoka.

Post Six was also responsible for encouraging the local Asmat to raid Koperapoka Village. The schoolteacher there, encouraged by the Japanese, was 'inciting the Papuans against our troops'. So, the Allies arranged for a looting-cum-spying party to visit Koperapoka. They looted and spied, reporting Japanese at Otakwa, Inauga, Aikwa, Koperapoka, Atuka, Timika and Kekwa Villages. Other information brought back to Post 6 included the fact that the Japanese had abandoned Yapero Island and Kokonau due to Allied bombing, that barges were carrying supplies to Timika Village, and that 10 Japanese soldiers were stationed at Erev, but they only had native canoes at their disposal.

There were only two occasions during which the Japanese and Australian troops came face to face in a military engagement on the south coast of West New Guinea. Army Captain C. C. Wolfe who was in charge of a small ship called 'Rosemary' described the first one.

Just when the Rosemary expected to reach the Ipukwa [Tipuka?] River around the next bend, they saw two low barges, side-by-side, filled with Japanese soldiers, coming at full speed around the bend. The Japanese opened up with a heavy machine gun, mortar bombs along with rifle fire. The Rosemary responded with its forward gun manned by Cpl. Barbouttis who then hurled grenades at the Japanese barges. With a pair of pliers, Wolfe pulled out some cartridges that had gotten stuck in the rear twin guns and started firing. The Japanese went out of sight behind a bend. The wounded were then attended to with Felix Maturbongs handing out field dressings. Under the calm direction of the Asmat onboard, the Rosemary headed back to the Ambukera River, then downstream on the Atimet. Heading out to the open waters, Cpl. Barbouttis was buried at sea.

Then, on 30 January 1944, Post 6's commander, Lt. Roodakoff, called for immediate air support as the Japanese had begun an attack. Early the next day, three enemy barges approached Post 6, but the troops there attacked 'and we killed all the men – [then] five more enemy barges approached and shot up both banks of the river for one hour. We evacuated.' The barges left, as they were probably uncertain as to the position of Post 6. Later, the Allied air force 'reported that four barges were sighted in the vicinity of the mouth of the Lorentz River and were strafed and sunk'. It was estimated that some 60 Japanese had been wounded or killed at the engagement at Post 6.

At first, the Kamoro got along well with the Japanese. However, soon the invaders needed food and the Kamoro were forced to plant large gardens. Reluctant to work to produce food, paddle, or act as porters, they were punished by beatings and even death. There are tales of Kamoro men tied on the beach at low tide, then drowned slowly as the tide rose. The Kamoro also suffered from Allied bombings and were forced to witness the beheadings of captured Allied pilots. The war years also saw a marked increase in drunkenness from the consumption of palm wine. The end of the war was a relief for the Kamoro. They participated in the hunting down and killing of isolated Japanese under administrative encouragement but also for revenge.

The family canoe paddled by mum and dad, hold the children out of the sun. They set off on their daily task of seeking food for their sustenance.

THE POST-WWII PERIOD   6

The inland village of Iwaka. The houses were built by a lumber company that cut their forests for a pittance. The large village size shows that abundant natural resources are nearby.

Development proceeded slowly after the war years. Most of the Kamoro lived in a subsistence economy, with some possibilities for paid employment with the Dutch oil company in Sorong. At the village level, occasional Chinese traders came to exchange goods like tobacco and tools for crocodile skins, ironwood, and '*massoy*'. A ship run by the Roman Catholic Church plied the coastal villages on a regular basis, purchasing copra (dried coconut meat) and bringing essential goods at relatively low prices.

During the years just following WWII, many Asmat came to live in the Kamoro area to escape the more than usual devastating intra-tribal fighting and headhunting. This gave the opportunity for some priests, notably Father Zegwaard, to learn their language and customs, prior to serving as the first missionary in the Asmat area. The Kamoro did not receive the Asmat with open arms, remembering past headhunting raids and seeing their sago and other food resources seriously depleted. Eventually, the government arranged for the Asmat to return to their homes.

The end of the war saw intra-Kamoro fighting in the western part of Mimika, as well as a resurgence of rituals. Some western Kamoro villages moved to Omba where, with participating villages from Etna Bay, an important nose-piercing ceremony took place.

As part of the Dutch policy of self-determination, an effective if unofficial council was set up which included government officials and Roman Catholic teachers. This council was responsible for the yearly scheduling of activities. Their remit included the alternation of traditional rituals, work, and Christian celebrations. After 1954 this council was expanded to include some Kamoro as well as their Kei teachers. But the council's plans for development did not register much success. However, it did expand the vision of some influential Kamoro leaders as well as that of some young men.

Changes in the Roman Catholic Church

Momentous modifications took place in the Catholic Church when the order of Franciscans (abbreviated OFM) took over from the established Sacred Heart order (MSC) in the running of church affairs. While missionaries of the

Formerly, Kamoro social structure was based on a system of matriarchy. Some groups still reflect this grouping, although outside influences have created a patriarchy-based society.

MSC had begun to loosen up their prohibitions of various aspects of Kamoro culture, the arrival of the Franciscan's cultural understanding became more important in church policy. The MSC thought of their mission as necessary to bring development and civilization to justify the prohibition of some of the Kamoro practices while stimulating others. It was up to the priests to pick and choose what was forbidden and what was encouraged. By 1957, the government passed a 'feast ordinance' whereby some Kamoro rituals were allowed, but only after notifications were given. (Jacobs, 2011)

After the war, church philosophy shifted to the belief that if Kamoro society was to change, it could do so far more effectively if it could integrate some (and only tolerable) aspects of the native culture. Of course, the idea was to ease the Kamoro's assimilation of the Catholic religion. Thanks to the language and mythological research of Father Zegwaard and Father Drabbe, the Church had acquired an understanding of the Kamoro culture and mind sorely lacking in the past but essential to the new policies of the local mission. Thus, baptisms with holy water were connected with the initiation rituals and canoes made for the '*kaware*' festival were blessed by priests.

Along with the new theological flexibility shown by the Roman Catholic Church, there was a new willingness to encourage the carving skills of the Kamoro. They were urged to continue their art, albeit with a religious focus: Madonna and Christ incorporated into a traditional spirit pole, as well as figures of Christ on the cross.

Aside from these sacred carvings, the Franciscans also encouraged the Kamoro to make items for sale as plain souvenirs that included small ancestral figures, miniature spirit poles, walking sticks, items small and easy to transport. While local sales were few, the Church sent this type of carvings to Holland where it was sold to help the finances back in West New Guinea.

Another great change to the Catholic Church policy came as a result of the Second Vatican Council under the most liberal Pope John XXIII from 1962 to 1965. Among its many earth-shaking conclusions was that Christian rules should be adapted to local cultures or not imposed at all. One of the priests in Kokonau pointed out the difficulty to enforce the prohibition of pre-marital (and extra-marital) sex that the Kamoro found most difficult to accept. (Never resolved.) The first OSC priests conflated their moralistic teachings with a prudish western way of life, ignoring Christian moral failures in Europe, such as prostitution, debauchery, and out-of-marriage sex.

The mass was switched from Latin to the vernacular and the priest faced the congregation instead of facing away from the faithful. While a Papuan

*Families travel regularly either upriver or downstream and set up '**kapiri kame**' for as long as three weeks to make sago, hunt or fish, and gather mangrove foods to supplement their diets.*

priest came to Kokonau, there have been no Kamoro pastors, even to the present. But Catholic laymen did take part in church rituals, including the celebration of the Eucharist. I have attended mass where drums were played and young men strummed guitars to accompany the singing, and witnessed a number of instances where the Kamoro integrated Christian and other foreign influences into their lives and ceremonies.

The Catholic Church celebrated its golden jubilee in 1977 with a huge gathering of Kamoro, 9,000 of them according to one source. Bishop Tillemans was commemorated by having his figure carved on a large '*bitoro*' and given the role of a Kamoro figure from the time of the '*amoko*' ancestral heroes. Canoes were blessed en masse with drumming and singing stretching throughout a whole night. (Jacobs, 2011)

The Protestants try again.

In 1956 the first airplane landed at Kokonau, with the first European Protestant missionary family. The Evangelicals from the US, from a missionary organization called TEAM (The Evangelical Alliance Missions), attempted to wean the Kamoro away from the Roman Catholic Church. In the 1930s, Protestants from Ambon attempted the same thing but failed. They had no better luck in the 1960s. However, a book that in part covers this more recent attempt, *Incessant Drumbeat*, reveals some aspects of Kokonau at that time, not found in any other literature. (Lagerborg, 1994)

The TEAM missionary Larry Rascher with his wife and three children moved to Kokonau in the early 1960s. He replaced the departing missionary Lovestrand who left with his family. At the time, ships brought goods there only twice a year. There were 'only crocodiles, mosquitoes and sand flies in this melancholy place... along with snakes and poisonous lizards'. The town's population was estimated at 2,500. The Raschers lived for some six years in Kokonau before moving to the Sempan village of Sumapro. There, Larry Rascher was successful in planting the TEAM's evangelical interpretation of Christianity.

When the Rashers arrived in Kokonau, there were two other TEAM members living there. Doris Florin was the teacher in a one-room Protestant school. Phyllis Griffiths, a linguist, was attempting to translate the Kamoro language. When Doris Florin left Kokonau to get married, the linguist Mary

Stringer replaced her. Many Kamoro considered these unmarried women, as Larry Rascher's 'other wives'. TEAM had a difficult time: thanks to the influence of the Catholic mission, Protestantism was viewed as 'the false religion'. They had a better time of it away from Kokonau, where the Kamoro were 'more responsive to the gospel and less controlled' by the Catholic priests. At Amar Village, TEAM built a church, a school, and an airstrip. However, 'in Kokonau, harassment from the Roman Catholic hierarchy continued unabated'. (Lagerborg, 1994)

Before the arrival of TEAM in Kokonau, a retired policeman named Humassey from Ambon had started a small church for non-Catholic government workers. When the Raschers arrived, only one Kamoro was attending this Protestant church. But as time went on, their church drew more and more disgruntled Kamoro. Eventually, there occurred an inevitable split in Humassey's church with some following the Rashers' evangelical faith, and the others keeping to the mainstream Protestantism.

The Evangelicals were dismayed at the Catholic priests' practice of distributing tobacco, even to children, as a reward for church attendance. (A book about the highlands Christianity is entitled *No Tobacco, No Hallelujah.* [Smedts, 1955]) At the time, the Kamoro still used their fetishes, but secretly. The Dutch had banned the old initiation rite of filing a boy's teeth. Nearly everyone carved, according to the Rashers.

Evolution of Kamoro attitudes

The decade between 1960 and 1970 saw the change from Dutch control of West New Guinea to that of Indonesia. The Kamoro accepted this and there were no great upheavals. They accepted the compulsion to fly the Indonesian flag at all rituals and gatherings or face punishment. I saw the prominence of the nation's red and white flag at all the rituals I attended over the years, even in events for foreign visitors where many canoes were decorated and displayed in unison in a spectacular scene.

Under Indonesia, small-scale commerce, previously run by the Chinese, passed into the hands of the Bugis from South Sulawesi. A large-scale migration, begun under the Dutch, took place by the mountain Amungme to an area called Agimuga, located east of the edge of Kamoro/Sempan lands. Under the Indonesian rule, the migration ended up with many deaths due to malaria and none of the planned development taking place.

The Kamoro took the change from Dutch to Indonesian rule without objections. This was very much the opposite of the attitude of the Amungme and other groups in West New Guinea. They never joined the Organisasi Papua Merdeka (OPM/ Papuan Freedom Movement) rebels who have long fought and continue to fight for independence.

Dr. Jan Pouwer has traced the Kamoro attitude toward outsiders as an evolving phenomenon. At first, foreigners were often received with hostility, to the point of killing some of them. We do not know the reasons for this, as those who suffered but survived the aggression wrote all of our descriptions of these 'murders'. There are no Kamoro accounts as to why they killed outsiders. Perhaps, it was to avenge a previous kidnapping, or cutting down of precious coconut trees without permission.

During the next phase of contacts, the Kamoro became far friendlier and more obliging, as they sought much desired modern goods such as metal tools, clothing and tobacco. During this time, the western part of the Mimika area became the focus of exchanges, as outside merchants were reluctant to travel further east. Pouwer records the exchange of the skull of a relative for a handkerchief to show the degree of Kamoro desire for material goods from the outside world.

It is likely that this desire for outside goods contributed to the Kamoro's acceptance of the Dutch government, the Roman Catholic Church and schools. However, it soon became evident to the Kamoro that it did not become much easier to acquire modern goods. The acceptance of outsiders' control meant that there was drastic disruption of the traditional Kamoro lifestyle, as we have seen above. And there were taxes to pay, and forced labor for projects such as making of gardens, mostly for the benefit of outsiders. These factors led to disenchantment along with passive resistance and a degree of resignation.

This passivity led to outsiders' belief that the Kamoro culture and spirit had vanished. The bleakest assessment of the Kamoro comes from Father Trenkenschuh: 'Mimika strikes a person as a dead area filled with zombies. There is no work and no interest in work. Religion of the past is no longer celebrated and the Christian religion means nothing to the people. The past is gone forever. The present lacks vitality. The future holds no hope. ... This is a society without any pride in itself, and one, which totally lacks any sense of excitement and enjoyment of life. ... Infant mortality is still over 80 per cent and Mimika is filled with underfed and sick people. ... It has been almost 40 years since any local Mimikan feasts have been spontaneously celebrated....

By 1970 almost all local art had disappeared and all artists are old men. … The three successive governments and the missions have failed in every effort to promote any development in the Mimika area. … It was difficult for the mission to keep missionaries interested in the people and the area. From 1959 to 1969, East Mimika had 13 different pastors. The people never had a chance to know and trust the missionary…'. (Trenkenschuh, 1982). This very negative assessment has been widely and rightly disputed. (Jacobs, 2011)

While some elements of this most negative assessment might be true, it presents a very distorted picture of the situation of the Kamoro. The missionary priests, the pioneer proselytizers of the Asmat, saw what Europeans considered a most 'exotic' culture practicing headhunting, cannibalism, impressive ceremonies and ritual sex. By contrast, the Kamoro were a boring, tame lot, having passively accepted Christianity and given up many elements of their traditional lifestyle 30 years previously. And the Roman Catholic Church had evolved considerably in regard to just what was 'acceptable' in traditional cultures. Of course, the Kamoro suffered from being contrasted with the Asmat in the eyes of the missionaries and the world, taken with the dynamic, 'exotic' Asmat.

Freeport and the Kamoro: encouraging carving

The mining company Freeport Indonesia arrived among the Kamoro to begin its infrastructure work at the end of the 1960s. Some Kamoro were hired during this initial phase for various menial jobs. And the company port of Amamapare attracted many Kamoro who lived (and still live) on the nearby island of Keraka. The port, as well as the road leading to the mountains, (to the mine site in the highlands), were all built on Kamoro-owned traditional lands. There were benefits for the local Kamoro in free health services, a market for fish and mangrove crabs, as well work opportunities. Later, a company-financed long-term multi-million-dollar program compensated the local Kamoro for their territory that had been taken over for the port, the road, and the tailings deposition area.

Still-practiced Kamoro rituals required the skills of hereditary carvers for the making of the 'mbitoro', a winged totem-like pole with carvings of recently deceased important men. The carvers also continued to make drums. The arrival of Freeport workers produced a market for Kamoro carvings, unfortunately of the cheapest, low-quality variety.

In 1990, the company started the Yayasan Freeport Irian Jaya (Freeport Foundation Irian Jaya) for the 'development of Papua'. This foundation and its programs were begun thanks to a Freeport American staff member named Doug Learmont. He urged the company to pay attention to the Amungme and the Kamoro who lived in the area where the Freeport mine and its infrastructure were located. When I visited Freeport in 1985, there was not the slightest attention paid to the culture of the local Papuans. Indeed, some lived off the company garbage dump and some sold their wives and daughters for sex with Freeport employees. But one of the top Freeport officers, Mr. Paul Murphy, did pay attention to Mr. Learmont and funds were found for his development activities.

Under Mr. Learmont's direction, Freeport began the Bapak Angkat (Foster Father) program for the Kamoro, to foster the preservation and sales of their carvings. A Gedung Seni Kamoro (Kamoro Arts Building) was erected as a center for carving as well as demonstrations of cooking and sampling of traditional dishes. Freeport paid a stipend to the carvers to support their families and supplement any sales of their carvings to visitors. The carvers were also encouraged to make large standing figures of ironwood to decorate the fountain of the newly-built company hotel called The Sheraton named for the company that initially managed it.

Unfortunately, Mr. Learmont did not see the relative success of his efforts. For reasons of his own, he had become a member of the Muslim faith. (Perhaps his wife was a Muslim.) He was accused by some Papuans (not any Kamoro) of allying himself with Muslim Indonesians in the Company and coming between the American staff who wanted to help the locals and the needs of the Papuans as perceived by them. Some Amungme sent a letter of complaint (based only on hearsay) about Mr. Learmont and some Indonesian staff to Mr. Jim-Bob Moffett. Based on this letter, Mr. Learmont was unjustly forced to resign.

In 1995 Freeport went through a traumatic period when anti-company rioting both in the highlands and around company installations in the lowlands forced a closure of the mine operations for several days. Mr. Moffett arrived in his private jet and threw wads of cash to try to resolve problems he hardly understood. The Indonesian military had a hand in organizing the rioting, probably hoping for more financial largess from Freeport.

The riots marked the end of the Freeport Foundation for Irian Jaya Development (FFIJD), and replaced by the Lembaga Pengembangan Masyarakat Irian Jaya (LPM, Community Development Agency Irian

Jaya) and still other names, all best known as the one per cent fund as the company committed one per cent of its gross revenues to this fund. The board of directors included the '*bupati*' (the chief civil official of the district), Amungme and Kamoro representatives, members of the three most popular local churches and Freeport staff members. With many millions of dollars at its disposal, this organization was open to waste and corruption. In a later name change, it became the LPMAK (Lembaga Pembangunan Masyarakat Amungme Kamoro (Organization for the Development of the Amungme and Kamoro Communities), mostly run by Papuans. It continued to disperse huge funds from the Freeport's one per cent fund. The organization supported religious, educational, and economic development activities. Although seven tribal groups now living in the Timika area used the LPMAK funds, a disproportionate amount went to Kamoro (and Amungme) activities, as due to the area's traditional landowners. In the latest change, this body was undergoing another re-organization in 2020.

Another company-financed organization (LEMASA, or Lembaga Masyarakat Kamoro, Organization for the Kamoro Community), run by Kamoro leaders, disburses funds for various necessities such as the return of bodies of the deceased to their home villages from Timika. But internal corruption has been a brake on its efficiency.

Without the support from the Foster Father program, the Kamoro Arts Building kept on functioning as a carving production center thanks to other Freeport funding. In 1992, the well-known carver Timo Samin moved to the Kamoro Arts Building as one of its leading members. He left in disgust and anger in 1998 when other carvers blamed him for attempting to take control. After that this center and its carvers lost momentum and gradually disbanded, with the carved frontage of the building bought by Dirk Smidt, curator of the Rijksmuseum voor Volkenkunde in Leiden and shipped to Holland.

Freeport kept commissioning the Kamoro to make large carvings and decorations for its propeties and for public display. Beginning in 1998s, Freeport sponsored a series of large-scale Kamoro festivals where carvers had the opportunity to sell their production at excellent prices. These festivals helped the Kamoro to regain a degree of pride in their traditional culture. Unfortunately, these festivals stopped after a few years due to unreasonably increased costs demanded by the Kamoro organizing committees. (See the Chapter 10 below.)

After the termination of the large-scale festival, Freeport began under my urging, a program of purchasing carvings in the various Kamoro villages and holding a series of expositions in Jakarta, Tembagapura, Bali and other places. During these expositions, many carvings were sold, with the sale price going directly to the carvers. Small groups of Kamoro traveled to each of these events, holding carving demonstrations, along with chanting, dancing, and playing of their drums. The public's appreciation of these manifestations of Kamoro traditions helped to restore a degree of pride in their culture.

Aside from encouraging carving, various Freeport programs have helped the Kamoro in different ways. Most of these programs were specifically directed to the Kamoro whose lands were used by the mining company. They benefited disproportionately from Freeport largess, but some benefits also reached the Kamoro living further away. These benefits include near-free top-notch health care in an excellent hospital, educational and economic development programs.

Kamoro rituals are directed toward ancestral spirits, especially those recently deceased as shown on this large carving erected for an initiation ritual.

KAMORO RITUALS 7

One or two important recently deceased men are carved for initiation rituals and invited to participate in the festivities.

Early descriptions of Kamoro life mention a near-continuous cycle of rituals. Little is known first-hand about most of these celebrations, as they were – if not forbidden – then strongly discouraged by both the government and the church. We only have a glimpse of them from the BOU Expedition (see above), from Jan Pouwer, Father Zegwaard, and much later by myself. There were no blanket prohibitions on rituals, and only the nose-piercing part of the initiation cycle was forbidden, stated as for health reasons.

The cycle of the Kamoro festivities had and retained a dual purpose. They were partially directed at their ancestors, especially the important men who had died recently and whose spirits were honored. As these spirits retained for a while a great deal of power over their descendants, honoring them properly ensured good health and a plentiful material life. There were no recorded instances of rituals to honor or invoke any supreme being or any spirits aside from the ancestors.

The second purpose of the rituals was, and remains, social and economic. This brings into focus two essential Kamoro concepts: that of the '*aopao*' and the '*kaokapaiti*'. The '*aopao*' idea can be rendered as 'reciprocity' or 'exchange' in the wide sense of the terms. But this is not simply a give-and-take-and-give-back event. Exchanges are made over time and are often continuous, not a one-off affair.

Today, '*kaokapaiti*' is generally used as meaning 'in-law'. Its former meaning, still applicable to an extent today, was what was 'owed' to one's wife's family when no sister could be exchanged for the wife. This 'owing' meant not just in giving physical items, such as a canoe, but also labor for the wife's family. This resulted in the frequent move of the new couple to her territory or village, so that they could help her kinfolk. Today, the '*kaokapaiti*' figure prominently in the initiation rituals of the boys related to them by marriage from their wives' kinfolk.

The '*karapao*' initiation ritual remains the only ritual practiced regularly today. And most villages in the west of the Kamoro area have abandoned even this last remaining tie with their ancestral beliefs. The word '*karapao*' refers to both the ritual itself as well as to the special building erected for this purpose. Below, I will refer to the ritual with a capital K and the building with a lower-case k.

*Men who have the hereditary right to act as ritual drummers play together outside a '**karapao**' a structure specially built for an initiation ceremony. Ancestors are thus called to participate in the ritual.*

The 'Karapao's main purpose is the initiation of young boys into male adults. Over a period of some 20 years, I have assisted in segments of the 'Karapao' on several occasions, in five different villages. It is a ritual that can often take place over a one-year period with long phases of inactivity, until the leaders decide that it is time for the next stage. (See the chapter below)

Aside from the 'Karapao', I have only seen three other traditional rituals. One of these, called the 'opako kakuru' was to celebrate an unusually good breadfruit harvest in Mioko Village. The other took place in Iwaka Village and included a secret women's ritual along with the re-creation of the local phase of an important legend. At Ipiri Village I saw a short version of the 'kaware' that was formerly practiced as a rejuvenation, or life-enhancing ceremony. An even shorter version of the 'kaware' is now performed for visitors at Timika Pantai Village.

There were important rituals performed in the past. The little we know about them comes from the anthropologist Dr. Jan Pouwer who has written an extensive chapter about them. (Pouwer, 2003). He covers the 'emakame' in the west (called 'kiawa' in the east of the Kamoro area), relating to the female right emphasizing inner knowledge or 'mapere'. Its counterpart was the 'kaware', the male left, stressing outer knowledge, 'ipare'.

Pouwer wrote that the 'emakame' was the 'festival of life'. It included a spectacular richness of carvings and ornaments. The sculptures included ceremonial wooden boards called 'urumane' that featured the 'mopere' motif, shaped like an oval, a diamond, or a lozenge. This was the maternal vagina (or navel), the essence and source of all human life. Life-sized carvings of pregnant women were placed in front of the ritual structure representing the founding ancestral mothers of the 'taparu' that made up the main wards of the settlement where the ritual was performed.

The 'emakame' served to promote sexual behavior and procreation, and to emphasize ancestral descent, the commemoration and honoring of the dead. The literal meaning of the name of the festival is 'house of bones', which in the final stages, the bones and skulls of the deceased were discarded and left to decay. As in other rituals, gender antagonism was given vent by a free-for-all, mock war between the men and the women.

The male-oriented 'kaware' underlined the man's relations to the spirits. It emphasized male skills in holding secret knowledge that gave men power in all walks of life. Many new items were made for this ritual: canoes, paddles, drums, sago bowls and masks. All these items originated in the underworld and were brought up from there by an ancestor-hero named Muanuru. His character was definitely not admirable. The beginning of his journey came just after he had intercourse with his sister. Feeling somewhat ashamed, he found a waterlogged trunk that led him to the underworld. There our man saw all kinds of material things that the Kamoro did not yet possess. He tried to steal these items but was caught by a spirit whose name was also Muanuru. His sprit namesake imprisoned him in the arms of a large carving that held him tight, preventing escape. His brothers-in-law finally rescued him. They somehow found the thief and released Muanuru from the embrace-prison.

The '*Kaware*' ritual is meant to, at least, partially focus on the production of artefacts and the transfer of the knowledge of wood carving to the younger generation. I did not see any of this teaching of carving in the truncated version of this ceremony in 1996. The emphasis was initially on a ritual-play where the men pretended to be dead and one of their numbers went into a pseudo-trance. The emphasis was on the making of canoes and on the presence of spirits in the form of men wearing masks. I took many photos of this ritual, published in David Pickell's 2001 *Kamoro. Life Between the Tides*. Later, when I set up visits for foreign guests to Kamoro villages, where the men performed a part of a '*Kaware*', the spectacular decorated canoe 'parade' ending with the whole village in an enthusiastic final dance.

There are also ad-hoc traditional elements in various 'foreign' celebrations such as those connected in the past with the Dutch queen's birthday when her crown was carved in the wing extension of an ancestral spirit pole. Other such festivals included the Roman Catholic mass, Christmas, Easter, Christian funerals and even '*kabupaten*' (district) political elections. In most of these, the 'traditional' element is restricted to some of the participants wearing some non-western clothing, drumming, and chanting. During one election, some Indonesian political parties paid to have small '*karapao*' buildings erected in a village. And groups of Kamoro dancers are (relatively) often invited to government or company functions for entertainment. The non-traditional feasts are gathered under the designation of '*kakuru tena-we*', meaning celebrations for foreign people. Pouwer wrote that the Kamoro lived in two different worlds, their own and one in which they engaged with foreigners; and these were clearly separated. However, Kamoro myths and other narratives have now incorporated foreign elements, such as western goods in the shape of outboard motors and tools. An overall perspective comes from Harple (2000) in explaining that the Kamoro reacted to political and economic changes over time by engaging with these changes and incorporating them in their narratives.

Kamoro initiation: Father Zegwaard

It seems that in former times, the initiation was a multi-part affair. The first part took place for quite young boys, and this is the case today. The other parts, for boys at and past puberty, and physically developed young men, happened several years after the first one, but before marriage. As part of the ritual, the boys had to prove their capabilities in various activities such as fishing, hunting and the making of a canoe. Nose piercing, called '*mirimu kame*' was practiced at this stage.

We are most fortunate in having a description of a traditional initiation ritual by Father Zegwaard. This took place in Atuka Village in 1951. He wrote that the initiation was formerly a five-part ritual. But rituals only accompanied the first stage, for young boys; the second, for adolescents; and the third, for young men. The last two stages only referred to the transition to middle age, then to old age. Father Zegwaard wrote that the small boys were called '*ain-ru*', meaning 'little people with potential for growth'. The term '*mut-apoka*' referred to adolescents and meant 'provided with testicles'. After the nose piercing, the young men were called '*ko-apoka*'. Middle-aged men were called '*aiper-apoka*' and men with grey hair, '*per-apoka*'.

Kei teachers told Father Zegwaard that the adolescent initiation was a simple affair. The youths were dressed in several layers of aprons or skirts that hung from their waists to the ground. These skirts, made of sago palm leaves, were called '*tawri*'. Songs suggested that the '*tawri*' signified pubic hair, highly desirable for boys and girls alike.

It was the nose-piecing ceremony that turned adolescents into fully mature males. There has never been a previous or subsequent systematic study of this ritual. When Father Zegwaard saw this ceremony, it had not been practiced for some 20 years, as it had been prohibited since the 1930s. 'Yet enthusiasm for the feast still had not subsided'. The Kamoro of Atuka had grasped the opportunity that 'arose accidentally' to organize this ritual'. The entire village participated wholeheartedly and joyfully in the long-prohibited ceremony. Formerly, this ritual was celebrated on a regular basis, with the active participation of the whole community, including the spirits of the deceased.

Father Zegwaard wrote that at first all the candidates ran away into the jungle. Then their sisters' husbands, their '*kaokapaiti*' ran after them and caught them. The youths were coaxed back to the specially built ceremonial house where they lay down. Here their sago skirts were cut. The women were in hysteria, especially the youths' mothers and older female blood relatives. One of the brothers-in-law took a thin peg of razor-sharp hard palm wood and thrust it with force through the young man's septum. The hole in the septum was gradually enlarged using increasingly thicker wooden pegs measuring 25 to 50 cm in length. The number of brothers-in-law, up to ten, who had to hold the plug with both hands, one to two meters long, determined the span of these last pegs. After the piercing was completed, rolled-up tree leaves were inserted into the hole to prevent it from closing.

While the nasal septum was being pierced, copious amounts of blood flowed. The 'mothers became maddened by licking up great quantities of blood streaming down...'. Another priest referred to these women as 'female devils straight out of hell'. After the operation, the candidates had to summon their strength and courage to stand up and face the audience, to 'look at the public in the eye', before being taken to their family houses. Their noses swelled, high fever often followed, and many had difficulty in breathing and swallowing with general weakness from considerable loss of blood. I cannot help but to ask if these symptoms were always so drastic. Perhaps it was always so, but there are far more painful initiations elsewhere in West New Guinea as well as in other parts of the world.

Once the young men recovered physically, this phase of the initiation continued. Father Zegwaard divided the rest of the ritual into three phases: the farewell to adolescence, the final examination of masculine skills, and the display of virility.

This began in the 'u-kame' or the hair-extension house. There, the golden-yellow fibers of the sago leaves, some 15 to 20 cm in length, were braided into strands that were then plaited into the ends of the young men's hair, drooped over the back to reach the shoulders. Father Zegwaard thought that this display 'lent a certain glow... a radiance associated with myths and songs of heavenly bodies'. A number of other cultures in West New Guinea also featured hair-extensions, sometimes associated with warfare and headhunting. In Atuka, imitation hornbills were made of coconut fiber and tied onto the hair extensions. The candidates' brothers-in-law shot at these 'hornbills' with small darts while the boys squatted on their haunches and mimed the flying movements and imitated the chugging sound of the flying hornbill.

There was also a food ritual in which the young men ate a variety of soft foods, including one made with mussels that Zegwaard calls 'omo-k-upuku'. Today, during the 'Karapao', a type of food is sometimes made from bivalves mixed with sago, wrapped in leaves and grilled over an open fire. The priest wrote that 'the ceremonial eating of soft foods showed that they no longer belonged to adolescents, but in their manner of eating they were identifying with adult males'.

The 'sauna' ritual took place in a specially built house where hot fires raised the high temperatures. Prior to entering, the young men were 'painted from head to toe with white chalk [probably lime], black ashes and their buttocks decorated with large leaves'. From the outside of the sauna-house, women poured water onto their sons and brothers through an opening in the front wall. Inside, the candidates' brothers-in-law drank the water running down the young men's shoulders. This ritual was considered a sort of purification, to leave behind impediments such as negative influences and forces experienced during long journeys or through visits from strangers.

The demonstrations of their skills in the use of bows and arrows, the hunting spear and the fishing spear were the most important and practical part of the adolescents' initiation. These tests were essential before a young man could marry and become a full adult, and a father of children. A plank target was set up by the archers' guild for the bow and arrow test. The oldest man of this guild fired the first arrow, followed by his 'brothers and sons', then his sisters' sons. It is not clear in the text if these kinship terms apply to the candidates. There followed tests set up by the guild of hunting-spear throwers. The fishermen's guild threw a coconut in the water, representing a fish that the candidates had to hit with a fishing spear.

The candidates also had to learn how an adult young man must behave toward his mother and women in general. What Father Zegwaard recorded seems at odds with the importance of women in Kamoro society, so perhaps he only refers to a temporary behavior of the newly initiated men. He translates a Kamoro phrase as 'mother, give me sago, you with the red genitals'. The word '*maperapoko*' means 'red genitals' and according to Zegwaard is the swear word used by men when they want to exercise their masculine authority.

Body decorations, with insignia and attributes showing their physical maturity – and especially their virility – represented the final element of the initiation as recorded by Father Zegwaard, what he called the 'apotheoses' of the young men. The items were worn by the initiates in the nose and on the penis, as these two protruding body parts were believed to 'contain a high concentration of vital energy or life force. The items could include two pieces of a hornbill beak, or equal fragments of a seashell, or a combination of two pigs' tusks worn in the recently pierced nose. (The last two items are still relatively common among the Asmat but no longer worn by the Kamoro.)

The penis covering was another special item worn by the young men. Zegwaard wrote that the word for penis shell or penis sheath was '*kamare-po-ko*'. The word '*ko*' remains in common use today and refers to the worm-shaped mollusks called '*tambelo*' in Eastern Indonesia. The animal is found in some fallen mangrove trees. The definition for '*ko*' by Zegwaard is 'shining, gleaming, glittering', and as the common name for this special kind of mollusk much sought after as a delicacy by the Kamoro. The mollusk is called '*ko*' because of the thin, gleaming layer of slime on its skin, as well as the traces of this slime in the tunnels the mollusk leaves behind as it consumes the wood. The use of the word '*ko*' draws attention to the penis cover shell's glistening layer of mother-of-pearl, as well as to the gleaming skin of the bamboo stem. The bamboo penis sheaths, worn more commonly by inland groups according to Father Zegwaard, was made from the species called '*e'eke*', and ended in a small pair of human legs. Today, the Kamoro I have asked do not remember these bamboo penis sheaths. And, in all the drawings and photos of this type of penis sheath found in Kooijman's well-illustrated book, the bamboo penis sheaths are all captioned as having been collected only in the Sempan area.

The initiation ritual requires the hunting of wild pigs by the male relatives of the boys. This is a dangerous hunt as men are occasionally killed by enraged boars.

THE KARAPAO TODAY 8

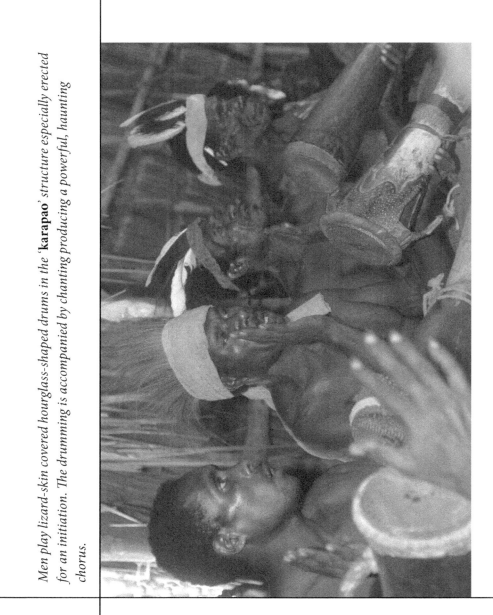

*Men play lizard-skin covered hourglass-shaped drums in the '**karapao**' structure especially erected for an initiation. The drumming is accompanied by chanting producing a powerful, haunting chorus.*

This boys' initiation ritual now (since around the 1990s) takes place in most central and eastern Kamoro villages every five to seven years. The following description comes from the various '*Karapao*' I have personally attended in different villages on a number of occasions. None of these were conducted exactly alike but there were many elements similar in all of them. There were also important variations.

When I began visiting the Kamoro in 1995 there were no references to any ceremonies in the recent literature. I had assumed that the Kamoro no longer held any traditional rituals. I was wrong. The following is based on my notes from the various '*Karapao*' rituals I witnessed.

The boys' ages undergoing this important lifecycle ceremony varied from about five to some 15 years. Once I saw a very young boy, perhaps only three or four years old, who participated for a while but was so scared and cried so much his father took him away. I was told that the boy would undergo the initiation the next time one was held in the village. Some Kamoro men told me that the 'ideal' age for the initiation was at or just before the beginning of puberty. When I asked why some of the boys were so young, the reply was that the ritual would make them into adults faster, implying a greater help to their families and their community. Most of the boys at the upper age range had for various reasons missed their '*Karapao*', such as being away from the village for an extended period of time (schooling elsewhere), sickness, because his relatives had not been sufficiently prepared, or that there were not enough boys in the village of the same age group to warrant holding the ceremony.

Shortly after beginning to visit the Kamoro, I stopped at Timika Pantai Village. While chatting with the '*kepala desa*', I heard some drums. "What's that?", I asked, "Getting ready for an initiation ritual", the village head answered. Taking a look, I saw a few men in a long, high thatched hut. Not much going on. They said for me to return when the initiation would reach its climax. "When would that be?" "Oh, in a few months". It took several trips, but it was very definitely worth it.

A dozen lizard-skin drums spoke with one voice as heavy-muscled men chanted a powerful, haunting chorus. The drumming stopped abruptly as the boys rushed out of the '*karapao*', the long, specially built ceremonial house. They wore all sorts of outlandish finery. The boys flung powdered lime

At the end of the initiation ritual, the boys wear their new finery and proudly ride on the shoulders of their sponsors, their uncles. Initiations in the past required several more phases, skipped in today's ceremonies.

into the air from bamboo tube containers. Riding on their male relatives' shoulders, the boys were surrounded by a shouting, joyous crowd, climaxing the year-long initiation ritual, the first one in nine years at this village. The ancestral spirits of the Kamoro culture on the south coast of West New Guinea must have been pleased. After several generations, the prejudice against the culture was making room for pride in the old traditions. Just in time too. A few more years of neglect and much of the ancient knowledge and customs of the Kamoro would have been lost forever. Now the culture has at least a fighting chance for survival.

Headhunting, cannibalism, and ritual orgies of heterosexual and homosexual persuasion. Many aspects of the cultures of the south coast of West New Guinea were forbidden by the outside world after its authority was established. The Kamoro did not follow the above practices in the subhead, aside, perhaps, for some heterosexual activities at the margins of (but not a part of) their rituals. Rather, the Kamoro ceremonies lost much of their importance due to semi-forced relocation into permanent villages, the obligation for increasing amounts of communal work, and the negative attitude toward their traditions by the Kei teachers and some of the priests.

At Timika Pantai, several days before the climax of the initiation ceremony, I thought I had stumbled on a headhunting feast. Groups of wide-shouldered men in graceful canoes were returning to the excited reception of their womenfolk who seemed to have thrown away their normal reserve, traded for uncharacteristic exuberance. That the men were carrying chunks of recently speared wild pigs seemed beside the point: their reception was straight out of Asmat headhunting accounts of the past. The male in-law relatives of the boy-initiates had returned from a successful pig hunt, essential for the continuation of the ceremonies. I could not help to but wonder if pigs had been substituted for humans? But there are no accounts whatsoever of cannibalism among the Kamoro, or even of headhunting. There are only descriptions of wars long past.

In many cultures, the taking of heads meant a spiritual and physical rejuvenation for the whole village, not only for the warriors. The ladies at Timika Pantai village certainly seemed rejuvenated. Elderly matrons were doing sexy steps, shaking various parts of their anatomy in a most youthful manner. While girls and young women would also dance, the leaders and best wigglers were undoubtedly the elder generation, perhaps remembering their past love conquests. Just about every day, some occasion or another would call for the whole female population of the village to dance back and forth in front of the '*karapao*' ceremonial structure where the men kept up an almost continuous pattern of drumming. Occasionally, the gentlemen would come out and join the ladies but most of the dancing was sex-segregated. Unlike in the past according to one informant, some sex took place during this ceremony. Perhaps loose behavior still happens, but out of the limelight.

The relatively staid behavior of the ritual was perhaps the leading factor in the seal of approval stamped on the ritual by the Roman Catholic Church. Father John, from Flores Island, stationed in the nearby town of Kokonau, arrived on a Saturday afternoon and took a long look at the ritual. He celebrated mass the following Sunday in a well-attended church. His long sermon, given plenty of attention, essentially stated that the Church today had no objections to the initiation ritual. On the contrary, it approved and supported the Kamoro traditions - a very different message from that of some of the early Roman Catholic missionaries and today's fundamentalist Evangelical Protestant churches.

There was another welcomed interruption of the initiation ritual. Freeport's malaria control team stopped by for several hours during two consecutive days to take blood samples from everyone willing to have a finger pricked, along with unwilling, screaming children whose parents wanted their kids tested. The malaria control team returned two days later to advise of the results as to who had malaria and what type, along with pills for this common but debilitating disease. Malaria reduces energy, productivity, and pleasure in life. In can induce life-threatening high fever. In the case of pregnant women, a bout of malaria can contribute to negative fetal development problems and delivery of low birth-weight babies with their much-reduced likelihood of survival.

Many Kamoro babies and infants, especially in isolated villages like Timika Pantai, still die of malaria every year. This is perhaps the reason why the boys are about seven years old before they undergo the initiation ceremony. By then, they have probably survived several bouts of malaria, building up at least a partial immunity to the disease. The underlying logic is that if the boys have survived childhood, it will not be a wasted effort to put them through the long and complex initiation ceremony.

Much preparation and effort went into the initiation rites whose final weeklong set of events climaxed a year of on-and-off events. Pretty much ignored before, during the last couple of days much attention was focused on the 58 boys, whose ages ranged from seven to fourteen years. Two to five boys from 19 extended families took part. Each of the 19 families took care to dress and decorate its crop of boys, competing with each other in the outlandish fashion category. There were no rules or judges, but all the families seemed very anxious for me to photograph their boys in the best finery available. All known traditions and cultures were fair play for enhancing the effect. As the base of the decorations, all the boys' bodies were painted with white lime-based patterns, and black soot, occasionally supplemented with colors of local vegetal matter. While these materials were available to everyone, the rest was a matter of preparation and investment. For me, one boy took the prize, at least in the cross-cultural extravaganza category: aside from his traditional patterns and colors, he wore the Christian cross, a bright Islamic red fez with Arabic writing and the most outlandish pair of over-decorated plastic sunglasses.

The pulse of the initiation ceremony could be felt in the '*karapao*' building. While the drumming seldom stopped completely, the choir of the hourglass shaped drums varied considerably in numbers and intensity during the initiation. The place was sometimes almost deserted, except for three or four men drumming and chanting. At other times, the '*karapao*' was full, over a dozen drums played with driving unison, making for an exciting, electric atmosphere.

The 50-meter long, high, narrow temporary structure remained the physical focus of the initiation ceremony. The front of the '*karapao*' was pierced with 19 doorways, one for each initiate and his family. With a thatch roof, the front on the building was covered with mats woven from strips of leaves. When the '*karapao*' was first erected, over a year ago, the mats had been painted with various animal designs. But these had faded during the months that various phases of the initiation had to be postponed due to other business at hand. But it could have been worse: while nine years had passed since the last initiation ritual here, at other villages the leaders told me that they probably will never have any traditional ceremonies anymore - implying that they were finished with the old, 'primitive' lifestyle. (This turned out to be wrong. I saw another '*Karapao*' at this village a few years later.)

That mentality is certainly understandable in the light of pressures in the past by teachers of the Roman Catholic Church and the government (both Dutch and Indonesian) to abandon their traditions. It is only relatively recently that this pressure no longer applies as the government and church have adopted a more tolerant attitude. And the fact that the large mining company operating in the area, PT Freeport Indonesia, has actually encouraged the Kamoro traditions by promoting their dances both locally and in Jakarta. It is still hard for some Kamoro to understand why, in the past, the outside world was dead set against their culture, but now things are different. Regardless, the first steps have been taken on the long road from the outsiders' prejudice to the Kamoro's pride in their culture.

When a sufficient number of young boys are ready for the 'Karapao' ritual, the village elders and the boys' families meet to decide when to hold this ceremony. Finding a proper tree for the carving of a 'mbitoro' (also called 'biro' in one village), the ancestral totem-like pole is next on the agenda. Tradition dictates the species of trees to be used, with a few kinds so designated. However, some villages are to use only 'their' own species. These trees must have wide plank roots that will form the upper 'wing' part of the 'mbitoro'. A designated group of men take their canoes to the forest to find the proper tree. Once it is found, they encircle around it, chant, and the 'kepala suku' throws lime on the lower part of the tree. This is a hereditary function. The plank roots are then cut off, except for one, and the trunk is severed just about its junction with the uncut plank root. This root is then cut just above ground level and the tree falls. All branches are then lopped off. The trunk with one plank root attached is then dragged to the nearest waterway. At the only time I saw this procedure, the tree was then tied between two canoes and brought back to an isolated spot very near the village with chanting and joyous shouts. No women or small children are allowed to witness this, nor the subsequent carving and painting of the 'mbitoro'.

A master carver, along with a number of assistants, carves the 'mbitoro' over several weeks. The man in charge outlines the major features of the 'mbitoro' and his assistants begin to hollow out the indicated spots. The main trunk or what will be the vertical section of the 'mbitoro' usually holds one or two large carved human figures. These represent important men who have died recently or revered ancestors. What will be the horizontal 'wing' or the uppermost section, the still attached plank root, is carved into various patterns with symbolic significance, usually of the natural world. At Iwaka Village, a most unusual 'wing' showed some 50 humans. These were the women and children who had died since the last 'Karapao'. I was able to obtain the names of each of these deceased persons. I was told that the village wanted to honor all of their recently deceased, and not only the two important men carved into the trunk. The families of these deceased made some sort of payment for each figure. While the carvers receive no monetary reward, the families of the boys to be initiated gave them food, drinks, and tobacco while they were working.

Once the carving is finished, the '*mbitoro*' is painted. The bulk of the painting is white, the coloring obtained from burned and crushed bivalve seashells. Other colors include red from the seeds of a wild fruit, and green made from rubbing of certain leaves. The black color, formerly from soot or charcoal, is now sometimes made from cheap carbon batteries, of the common Indonesian ABC brand. The night before the '*mbitoro*' was to be erected, the master carver 'opened' the eyes of the ancestor figures carved in the trunk by dotting them with paint.

The '*karapao*' is an elongated structure, its horizontal dimension depends on the number of boys who are to be initiated. Mangrove poles made up the framework of the '*karapao*'. Sago leaves serve as thatching for the roof, the sides and the front of the '*karapao*'. The roof slopes upwards from about a meter in the back to some eight or ten meters in the front. Mats, with crude animal drawings in charcoal, are hung on the vertical front part of the building.

The day of the erection of the '*mbitoro*' in front of the '*karapao*' marks the initial public phase of the initiation ritual. The completed '*mbitoro*' is revealed to the women and children. It is paraded around the village, sometimes with a man riding on it. Men and women dance near the large carving, shouting with joy and waving their arms. Supported by strong men, the '*mbitoro*' is thrown upwards, and then caught again. I was told that this movement of the '*mbitoro*' was not directed by humans but by the spirits of the important men whose figures had been carved into the trunk. These movements of the '*mbitoro*' testified that the spirits of the recently deceased elders had entered their carved wood bodies of the '*mbitoro*'.

After the '*mbitoro*' had been taken around the village, it is planted in the ground in front of the '*karapao*'. During several occasions I witnessed a '*karapao*' ritual, where young men were hidden in this hole, covered by sheaths of leaves. When the sheaths were removed, the men in the hole acted as though they were dead, some with tongues hanging out. Crying women danced near them as the men slowly came back to life and left their hole. The lower end of the '*mbitoro*' was then placed into the hole and it was pushed upright with long, forked poles. Once upright, everyone danced in front of the '*mbitoro*'. Some men climbed part of the way up the '*mbitoro*' and gave speeches, while the audience stopped dancing and listened. Thus ended the first phase of the initiation ritual.

The final phase of the initiation takes place several months, or even a year or more, after the completion of the '*karapao*' and the erection of the *'mbitoro'*. In some villages, intermediary rituals take place, with a number of important differences. I have never followed the complete *'Karapao'* cycle in any one village, as the intermediary events can happen any time and I did not live in any one village long enough to see them. On several occasions, I was advised that the *'Karapao'* would take place, but these invitations only referred to the initial or final phases, the most important ones. It was only on a very few occasions, and only by chance that I glimpsed some of these intermediary phases. On one occasion my wife Jina was able to film for one week during a period leading up to the final phase of the *'Karapao'* in Mware Village.

A new art form created with a tragic scene: a crocodile seizes a woman while she was net-fishing with a friend. The carver of this piece, Ponsi Amani of Mware Village, was killed by a drunk Kamoro in a nearby village. He was one of the best carvers.

KAMORO ART: REVIVAL, EVOLUTION AND COMMERCIALIZATION

9

A young carver, Frans Kupakoreyau of Timika Pantai Village displays a fine open fretwork shield. After working with an older master carver, Frans began making his own pieces only a few months before I purchased this excellent artwork.

The art world at large has yet to become aware of the fine woodcarvings of the Kamoro. Their next-door neighbors, the Asmat, have long overshadowed Kamoro carvings. Unlike the Asmat, the Kamoro carvers had little encouragement, or promotion for their traditional work until the 1980s. The Roman Catholic Church did encourage the carving of religious subjects, along with souvenir-type sculptures for some local sales and marketing in Holland for mission finances.

The former Dutch government and current Indonesian officials did not promote the work of the Kamoro carvers. Keen on civilizing and educating the Kamoro, there was no encouragement for the traditional culture and its associated woodcarvings. The carving tradition was moribund but far from dead. The inspiration and talent for fine works of art had not completely disappeared. Kamoro art experienced a partial revival, thanks to the efforts of a few employees of Freeport Indonesia, and the generous release of well-directed funds by the company.

After the mining company began its infrastructure work in the late 1960s, some workers purchased Kamoro carvings as souvenirs. Cheap and small were the main criteria, so the only carvings sold were quite crude and often badly made. This began to change in the 1980s.

We have seen in Chapter 6 how Freeport's encouragement of Kamoro art first developed thanks to Doug Learmont. I started working for Freeport while Learmont was still with the company. At first, there was other company employment for me and my interest in Kamoro art began only several months later. This was definitely not my initial job description but it evolved over the years as the company acted on its social responsibility to the Kamoro, the landowners of the lowlands where the company built a part of its infrastructure as well as where it deposited the tailings from its ore-concentrating mill.

For many years I had been interested in what was then called 'primitive' art, now going under the 'tribal' (and other) designation. I had bought woodcarvings in Africa in the early 1960s and eventually sold them in the US and Europe. In the New Hebrides (now called Vanuatu) I also brought and sold many objects I was able to find in remote areas where traditional cultures were still followed.

The first samples of Kamoro art I saw did not lift their art in my admiration. Crude hollowed-out figures with a caricature of a face and no artistically redeeming qualities. At least they were cheap. It took a while, but very slowly I realized that there was more to Kamoro art than these awful little pieces of junk. I saw a collection of stylized shields that some Kamoro had made that were going to Japan on exhibit. The pieces blew me away: a combination of abstract asymmetrical geometric patterns with great use of a few natural colors combined to enhance the relief. I had no idea where the carvings came from or how to obtain some for myself. But I knew that these Kamoro carvings were of exceptional, world-class quality.

Some western experts and collectors of tribal art refuse to accept the validity or authenticity of contemporary carvings from various traditional art-producing groups, famed for their work prior to abandoning their old ancestral religion. Their basic argument focuses on the changing inspiration of the carvers: the animist religion of the past verses commercialism today. They have a valid point when we look at some fine old pieces compared to crude contemporary copies. But while this is the case in many tribal areas, the argument is only partially valid for contemporary Kamoro art.

After several years of working with the Kamoro, I have realized that there were no high-margin ancient carvings still lying around. A drum made a decade ago is already considered old. The only really old Kamoro pieces, mostly in British and Netherlands museums (especially in the Rijksmuseum voor Volkenkunde in Leiden, Holland) were collected by various Dutch expeditions starting in 1828. The more recent pieces were sent back by Dr. Jan Pouwer who spent three years studying the Kamoro in the early 1950s. At the request of Dirk Smidt, then curator of Oceanic art at the Rijksmuseum, I contributed Kamoro carvings to this museum. (For collecting Kamoro carvings in the past, see Karen Jacobs' 2011 book, *Collecting Kamoro.*)

At one time Freeport considered setting up its own museum for Kamoro art. The company contacted the Smithsonian Institution in Washington D.C. with the possibility of a collaboration to jointly exhibit Kamoro carvings. The Smithsonian sent out a keen and enthusiastic young man, Todd Harple, to work on this project. However, the museum was never built due to the high costs that Freeport was unwilling to cover. Harple stayed for a couple of years, after which the company gave him funds for his studies in Australia, ending up with his PhD dissertation about the Kamoro. (Harple, 2000)

Reviving Kamoro art

For several years I had attended the yearly Asmat art auction in Agats, sponsored by the Roman Catholic Church, as a judge in the art competition. Thanks to the organization by Paul Murphy, a high-level Freeport executive, the company flew a few of us who were interested in Asmat art (from Timika to Agats) so we could attend this event.

At one of these auctions, I asked Mr. Murphy why Freeport did not sponsor something similar for the Kamoro. He thought for a short while and then said 'Yes, I agree, we should do it. And you organize it!' I hadn't expected that and the thought of the logistics involved made me blanch. But eventually, I did establish a festival and art auction for the Kamoro. (See Chapter 10 below, The Yearly Kamoro Kakuru Festival.)

By the late 1990s, better wood sculptures of the Kamoro were beginning to make a comeback from their long-neglected status. Their art had started to re-acquire the dynamic quality of the past that had been in imminent danger of being lost forever. Of course, there is no going back to the old days, before the government and the church imposed themselves. Within a relatively strict framework of different types of carvings, the art was inspired by the traditional religion of animism and respect for mostly ancestral spirits. While some elements of the old religion remain today, the incursion of the modern world has changed the world of the Kamoro art.

Types of Kamoro art made today

Today's Kamoro carvings do not have a single source of inspiration but run the gamut from the ancestral religion to pure commercialism. I was able to obtain an invaluable source about traditional Kamoro carving from a book by Simon Kooijman's, *Art, Art Objects and Ritual in Kamoro Culture*. This was a vital aid in acquiring a basic understanding of the traditional forms of Kamoro art. With the book at hand, it was easy to determine what was done in the old style and what was new. The book was illustrated with many black and white photos of museum pieces, brought back to Europe by various expeditions, starting in 1828 and ending with items sent by Jan Pouwer in the early 1950s during his fieldwork there. In order to encourage the Kamoro to continue carving in the traditions of their ancestors, I made photocopies of this well-illustrated Kooijman book and distributed them

The projecting 'wing' of an ancestral totem pole displays all the men, women and children who died since the last initiation some seven years before. This is the most elaborate wing carvings ever made.

among carvers of many villages. While later I could recognize some of the motifs and general shape of the old carvings, there was seldom an exact copy from a book.

It must be pointed out here that seldom has a Kamoro ever carved the same item twice. On several occasions, when more than one buyer wanted the same carving, I took the piece back to man who produced the object in the first place and asked him to make an exact copy: impossible. Not only that, but the attempted copies of the original were invariably bad. So I gave up these attempts at copying and can truly say that each carving is a unique piece. The inspiration, or whatever it takes to produce any carving cannot be repeated. This is the exact opposite of most examples of Balinese carvings where very competent craftsmen repeat a beautiful and/or clever piece of work ad infinitum.

The Kamoro carvings produced today result from a combination of ancient traditions relating to basic forms and style, mixed with a degree of commercialism. Some carvings are still part and parcel of the old way of life: tall ancestral statues ('*mbitoro*'), and drums ('*eme*') are both still required for the boys' initiation rituals. Other items, such as an almost endless variety of stylized shields ('*yamate*'), are no longer used for rituals (except on only two occasions), but the basic forms are maintained and the items are continually being made, albeit only for sale. The same combination, of the traditional form and commercial quality, applies to small ancestral statues ('*wemawe*') as well. Large masks called '*mbiikao*' formerly used in funerary rites are still occasionally made now.

The traditional colors used in Kamoro art have remained basically the same palette: red, white and black. The red is annatto, a sticky orangey-red substance covering the seeds of the *Bixa orellana* tree. White is made from burned and crushed shells ground to a fine powder and mixed with water. Black requires charcoal or soot as a base, mixed with water prior to application. For this black color I've seen the Indonesian ABC carbon batteries cut open and the black contents applied directly to carvings. Some colors bought in stores are of recent use.

The types of carvings described below appeared in a book on Kamoro art. As written by Simon Kooijman, the various art objects are placed in a ceremonial context, with legends incorporated where appropriate. A common feature in much of Kamoro art, we find the '*mopere*' motif. We have briefly mentioned this in Chapter 7 as a roughly oval or diamond shape, representing the maternal navel or vagina, the essence of life.

A fine shield with a geometric pattern being displayed at a festival. Shields are the most popular of traditional carvings now made for sale, as they make excellent wall hangings.

It is found anywhere in a carving, especially in the locations of the articulation of the human body such as the joints at the elbows and the knees. (Kooijman, 1984)

In our descriptions below, I have mostly relied on my personal experience with these art forms during the 20-odd years I worked with Kamoro artists. The main types of Kamoro carvings, art and decorations are as follows:

'*Mbitoro*' (also called '*biro*' but only in Pigapu Village): totem poles

The '*mbitoro*', ceremonial spirit poles, are the biggest and most spectacular of traditional Kamoro carvings. They vary in height from miniatures of less than 40 centimeters on up to ten meters. As with the '*yamate*', we can see a similarity with the Asmat culture, where the '*bisj*' poles have a somewhat similar form and function. In both cases, the carvings are used in rituals and represent recently deceased ancestors. One, two, and up to three people, their bodies standing on top of each other, make up the framework of the '*mbitoro*', with a large, open fretwork wing projecting upwards from the top portion of the sculpture. While the body of the '*mbitoro*' is carved out of the trunk of a mangrove tree, one of the broad, flattish buttress roots becomes the upward projection or wing: the tree is turned upside down in the finished sculpture. Aside from paying homage to one or more recently deceased respected elders, the '*mbitoro*' also holds the pride of place during the initiation ceremony where it is erected in front of the '*karapao*', the large structure specially constructed for this ritual.

'*Yamate*' or shields

The '*yamate*' are ceremonial and ornamental shield-like boards, with an overall shape that is either flat or with a slightly convex outer surface. The '*yamate*' falls into two types: solid with mostly geometric low relief decorations, often symmetrical but sometimes not; and open, flat, two-dimensional carvings with geometric fretwork, at times complemented by a human figure and/or a bird or dragon head. This second open type of '*yamate*' featured open motifs called '*à jour*'.

The first type, the solid '*yamate*', originates from the area east of Kokonau while the open types come from the west. Kooijman, quoting Pouwer, states that "In essence, the '*yamate*' were ancestor figures; each one represented a fellow villager who had died recently and bore the name of that individual." The '*yamate*' was formerly used in the '*emakame*' ritual, "as a symbol of both life and death, the genesis of life from death [as] the primary purpose of the ritual was the renewal of life." (Kooijman, 1984) It is likely that the yamate took its form and function from early shields, a fact brought out by the resemblance to the Asmat word for the 'real' functional shield, '*yames*'. The Asmat shields are always made with a functional handle, missing in the Kamoro '*yamate*'.

Many '*yamate*' today show carvings illustrating ancestral stories. A dragon of some sort appears frequently, with a monster ready to or just starting to devour a human. While these days the monster is called a Komodo by the carvers, the only large lizard found in the area is the long but (relatively) thinner-bodied *Varanus indicus*, not the massive bulk of the *Varanus komodoensis*. There was a larger carnivorous lizard running around in prehistoric Australia, the awesome seven-meter *Megalania prisca*, but that beast has been extinct for thousands of years. Ancestral memories passed down? Be that as it may, in a widespread Kamoro legend, a monster (dragon, snake, sometimes a crocodile) eats everyone except a pregnant woman who flees and hides. She gives birth to a son who eventually slays the evil monster and cuts it open. Out of the monster come all the ancestors of the Kamoro, as well as those of all the other human races.

'*Eme*' or drums

In the Kamoro culture, as in some other traditional Papuan societies, '*eme*' were, and still are used to call the spirits, ancestral and perhaps others. A mythical hero was also brought back to life by drums. In today's ceremonies, drums are used to call ancestral spirits during the initiation rituals. The Kamoro make their hourglass-shaped drums by burning out the insides of a section of a tree trunk. This is a delicate process that requires skill to make the sides just thin enough for light weight and good vibrations but without burning through. The open top part or head of the drum is covered with a stretch of reptile skin (from the mangrove monitor lizard, *Varanus indicus*), bound to the wood by a mixture of chalk from burned shells and human blood from the husband of either a sister or a daughter (formerly: exclusively) - but today, anyone's blood will do. Dabs of '*dammar*' pitch stuck on the lizard-skin drumhead are held close to a fire to tighten the skin for the desired sound. The drums often feature a handle carved as a man with a human face and a stylized body, or sometimes a fish. The top part of the drum has incised geometrical patterns (one carver told me this represented vines and leaves) that sometimes went all around the body of the '*eme*'. Other geometrical designs represent various animals, elements of nature and the human figure.

'*Wemawe*' or ancestor figures

Standing human figures come in a wide variety of forms and functions, grouped under a category called '*wemawe*'. Originally, these carvings were ancestral family protector figures, meant to guard a family against disease and other misfortune, as well as to provide success in their endeavors. These figures are carved with hollowed out insides, leaving only a cage-frame of limbs surrounding an empty space where the inner torso would be. The empty space and the closed eyes represented by the eyelashes show that the soul and spirit of the person have left. As in many human carvings, the figures are in a stylized sitting position, with elbows on knees and hands holding a staff or shield in front. But a variety of forms abound, some two dimensions, some in three. The best ones show strong facial impressions conveyed with powerful shapes and lines. This type of Kamoro carving had found the excellent sale value with outsiders and many were mass-produced as cheap deals to early Freeport employees. However, a number of these pieces carved later were excellent. Through the company's support, large two-three meter tall '*wemawes*' were commissioned to decorate different areas of the property which led to local government agencies following suit.

'*Mbii-kao*' or sprit masks

I first saw a man wearing a '*mbii-kao*' ('*mbii*' = spirit; '*kao*' = skin) in the mid-1990s when the men of Ipiri Village performed a much-shortened version of the '*kaware*' ritual (upon request) when these masks were worn. (Well described in David Pickell's *Between the Tides*.) The elders of Ipiri Village told me that it had been well over 40 years since the spirit mask had been used in a ceremony in the coastal area. The children of the village where certainly not used to the mask: when they caught their first glimpse of the mask-clad spirit figure, all fled for their lives in absolute terror.

Kooijman wrote that the Mimika area produced two types of '*mbii-kao*' masks. Both forms are made over a basic rattan framework. One category, called '*mamokoro*' features a long forward projecting snout and ends in high, pointed heads. They are made of vegetal fibers plaited into elaborate head-and-shoulder coverings with strips of grass below to conceal the lower body of the man representing a spirit. We found out that none of the older people at Ipiri knew how to make these masks, but that a young man had learned the skill from his grandfather before the old man died. He was the only person within several nearby villages that could still make a '*mamokoro*'.

In order to encourage the making of these masks, we created a category for them in the Kamoro yearly festival art competition. During one of the early festivals, three old masks, and two new ones were brought in, the latter especially made for the festival. The lead performer of one of the dance teams wore one of the new masks. We hoped this would revive the use of the 'mamokoro' in the Kamoro culture: after all, this was one of the main purposes of the Kamoro cultural festival. Unfortunately, this did not happen. However, a number of carvers made various wood figures, some flat and some three dimensional of men wearing the spirit mask. These sold quite well at the yearly festival.

I never saw the other type of 'mbii-kao' used in any rituals. But I did see a few of them and found out that they were only made by the Sempan, and named by them 'teeke waepuri'. While Kooijman maintains that these masks come from the eastern part of the Kamoro area, I have only seen them in the Sempan region. They are also quite similar to the ones made and worn by the Asmat. In a widespread myth about the origin of both types of these masks, it is recorded that the Kamoro migrated from the east to the west. So perhaps they were never made or worn in the present Kamoro area, only to the east. This type of 'mbii-kao' looks like a helmet with wooden decorations covering the outside of the eyeholes. The mask covers only a short section of the upper chest and large tubular sleeves for the upper arms. Both types of masks are worn over strips of sago palm leaves covering the torso and the legs of the performers, leaving the arms and feet exposed.

Pouwer mentions this type of mask, one without the long chin and large eye slits with wooden flaps. He wrote that a man from the eastern Mimika area had just introduced this type of mask to the central Kamoro area. I have seen similar masks but only made by both the Sempan and the Asmat where I purchased a few of them.

A few years after the ceremony at Ipiri Village, I saw masks used during an initiation ceremony at Iwaka Village. Several men there still knew how to make masks. The 'mamokoro' made there sometimes came with sheet-bark covering the rattan frame, while others covered the frame with woven vegetal matter. The quality varies considerably, depending on the ability of the mask-maker and time and care given. While in the old days these masks were made only by mask-maker with the traditional rights to do so, many other men made them as well while I was working in the area. During those years, I purchased several of these masks at Iwaka as they could occasionally be sold during the Freeport-sponsored Kamoro programs I organized in Jakarta, Bali and the company towns of Tembagapura and Kuala Kencana.

KAMORO ART: REVIVAL, EVOLUTION AND COMMERCIALIZATION | 107

'*Mbiikao*' masks were used in the past during funerary rituals, now no longer performed. Pouwer witnessed one of these in the mid-1950s. He wrote that men wearing these types of masks danced on a spirit platform called '*mbii-kawane*'. The purpose of the performance was to ensure that the spirits would retire to their designated homes, far away in the mountains, unburdened by any debts to the living. The masked men representing spirits leave the platform on their own accord after they have been told that their descendants no longer need their help. This was quite different from a ceremony I saw among the Asmat where the man and boys drove the 'helmet'-wearing spirits away into the jungle with blows and short spears.

A legend recounts how these masks first appeared. A spirit woman and a human woman both gave birth to sons at the same place and at the same time. The spirit woman asked the human one to raise the two children together. The boys grew up quickly and developed into frightening, impressively strong men. The local villagers were afraid of them, so they left and traveled to the west. There they found the lands were much more fertile than in their home to the east where they were born. The two men returned to their home village to obtain help to drive out the people living in the better lands to the west. Everyone prepared for war. While the two men were fishing, they saw spirits in the water celebrating a '*kaware*' ritual, wearing masks. The man who was the son of the spirit woman dove in the water where he met his spirit mother. She gave him a mask, along with another one for his human 'brother'. These were called '*mamokoro*'. (In another version of this legend, one of the brothers received a helmet-type of mask.) The two men wore these masks in the following war and thanks to the fright the masks inspired, the people living in the better lands were defeated and driven away. The two men died in the battle. Later, when the humans held their own '*kaware*' ritual that brought a renewal of life, masks were worn to honor the two men that had led the fight to obtain better lands.

Father Zegwaard wrote that masks were used in a funerary ritual when the celebrations reached their climax with the bones of the dead collected and stored in woven bags in a special ceremonial house called '*watani kame*'. He also mentioned that the masks were used to promote the growth of sago. These masks were preserved from one generation to the next and continually re-used. Thus in the past, they were difficult to purchase and collect.

(For much more information on the spirit masks, see Jacobs, 2003, and Pouwer, 1956)

'Otekapa' or walking sticks

Many of the items in the creative carvings category were walking sticks, items already made for sale at least by the 1960s and perhaps earlier. According to Kooijman, 'a walking stick could not have been made in the traditional culture. This was an item produced for sale to European travelers and represents a new commercial application of traditional motifs and traditional woodcarving.' Walking sticks are well carved, and now occasionally show a degree of real creativity. Catholic missionaries originally encouraged the carving of walking sticks topped with religious motifs and today the Kamoro sometimes carve bishop's staffs as walking sticks.

Animals

Animals were also placed in the creative carvings category. Freestanding animals were seldom a traditionally carved item. I saw hornbill-like headpieces worn at a dance and these items have long been known. The bird illustrated is the Papuan (or Blyth's) hornbill, *Rhyticeros plicatus* named '*komai*' by the Kamoro. As these birds mate and pair for life, they represent fertility and love for the Kamoro

An occasional cassowary, *Casuarius casuaris* to ornithologists, made an appearance on various carvings. The largest of the three species of this genus, the Kamoro calls the lowland cassowary '*petu'u*', '*monako*' or '*potere*'. The large, flightless bird stands at 1.7 meters and can weigh 60 kilograms; it is the largest of all endemic land animals in New Guinea. This colorful three-toed bird sports razor-sharp dagger nails. The middle toe is armed with a blade that can easily eviscerate a careless hunter. The bird's glossy black feathers made sought-after headdresses and dancing skirts for the Kamoro as well as highlands Papuans.

These and other animals began appearing at the Kamoro Kakuru festivals and became popular with visitors. While some of the representations were awkward at first, animal-type carvings have improved considerably, with fish, birds and crocodiles competing for attention. Carvers have even tried animals such as sago grubs and caterpillars. Some of these gems are as imaginative as any modern sculpture.

Daily life objects

'Pekoro' or sago bowls

The '*pekoro*' or sago food bowls were made in the past with a fair amount of care and carving, then these items went out of style with modern plastic replacements. But they have made a comeback now with a wider variety of shapes, often with more elaborate carvings than in the past. As carvers became aware of buyers' preferences and tastes, more carvings were added as well as human figures as handles. Lids were supplemented and the overall shape sometimes became a turtle or stingray with a long tail. Thanks to their small size and being flat, the '*pekoro*' were easy to carry and pack, thus popular with buyers. One of the best of these sago bowls, already unusual as it was the only one with a lid, was presented at a festival as carved by a woman, the sole lady who ever 'participated' in the traditionally male preserve of wood carving. This turned out a successful hoax (since it was her husband who was the carver), but it worked as the auction price of 'her' bowl sold for a higher price than the other '*pekoro*'.

There are two types of canoes made: the river canoe of the east, called '*ku*' and the one made for the ocean, the '*torpa*', used in the west. In the realm of items of everyday use, a few canoes are still adorned with relief carvings along with the upper parts of the sides. Occasionally, a male figure in high relief is carved near the prow of the '*ku*' while the female equivalent rises near the stern. These ancestor figures are meant to protect their descendants, the canoe's occupants. It was only once, in the Sempan village of Pece that I saw an ornamental fretwork extension mounted on the bow of a canoe. The canoes that participated in the '*kaware*' demonstrations for visitors were always much decorated with paint and leafy plants, but never with the prow extensions as shown in Kooijman.

'*Ku*' or Canoe and '*Po*' or Paddle

Canoes were difficult items to sell, due to their weight and large sizes: 7 to 15 meters. But the long carved paddles 'po' were purchased often. Paddles with carved blades slightly concave for men (and called '*werepo*') and slightly convex for women, (called '*kaokapo*') are still made for everyday use and sometimes sold in spite of their length (2.5 to 4 meters).

'*Wapuru*' or Sago pounder

An adze-like instrument, used for rasping sago, the '*wapuru*' featuring a little carving, was made in the past. Today we can find some miniature ones, elaborately carved but made only for commercial reasons. Full-sized used ones, with some carving, are occasionally offered for sale thanks to a few recent purchases.

'Anyaman' or ladies' plaiting

There was one category especially reserved for the ladies: vegetal fiber plaiting of either clothes or any daily use items. The grass used for this purpose is scientifically known as *Fimbristylis dichotoma*. Although we saw the odd basket, just about all the women who participated had made clothing: blouses (some with very sexy and fashionable, squared off shoulders and with small open slits in the front) and two-panel skirts, caps, and with a variety of body decorations. Withered but spry little old ladies with bright eyes and wonderful expressions held their woven items up during the auction, received their money, and, later, the top three graciously accepted their winnings in the evening.

Unfortunately, the skill of plaiting has been lost especially for the women living close to sources of plastic goods. Only the very old women were still able to produce a good variety of beautifully crafted objects like baskets, bags with straps and large mats. The more experienced plaiters incorporated a variety of complicated designs in the weave each with its own name, for example, the 'caterpillar eating the leaf' pattern.

The wearing of bark cloth has mostly gone out of style. But the making of it is still remembered. I asked a Kamoro group to make some for me. They did so and produced some fine examples after I photographed the process. They told me that they used two kinds of bark, from a mangrove tree called '*pako*' (*Rhizophora mucronata*) as well as from the '*tutu*' tree that I was not able to identify. Kooijman wrote that it was the inner bark of the Ficus genus trees that was used. The Kamoro gave me their name for bark cloth as '*tapena*' and '*uruna*'. Another group of Kamoro told me that bark cloth was formerly made from '*iwae*' (*Hibiscus tiliaceous*) or '*teh*' (*Gnetum genemon*).

The BOU Expedition reported that many Kamoro went about completely naked. Yet Kooijman's book shows many photos of penis cases made of bamboo, with many kinds of incised decorations. This author wrote that young men wore them after they had completed the initiation rituals. However, no photos exist of anyone wearing a penis sheath. Wollaston, a member of the BOU, wrote that older men sometimes wore a large shell on the stomach with the penis' foreskin tucked under it. Women were bare-breasted and wore a small piece of bark cloth or a narrow strip of grass or some other vegetal matter.

I tried to encourage the making of small body decorations for easy sales. These included the traditional men's armbands of plaited rattan, with tufts of cassowary feathers and fancy headdresses of rattan decorated with bird-of-paradise plumes if/when available. Four-pronged combs were also made for sale. The armbands sold relatively well, the combs and headdresses less so.

Surprisingly, some Kamoro weapons were snatched up by buyers. Spears with bamboo (or occasional bone) blades often remained unsold as buyers preferred the reworked iron blades which had seen real action in hunts for wild pigs, crocodile and cassowaries. We did sell a few war clubs made of hard wood. The old war clubs with a stone at the business end were usually not available for sale. While a few had hard stone blades traded from the highlands, most Kamoro stone axe heads were of softer limestone or sandstone from the far western Kamoro area where the mountains reached the sea. These stones were shaped like pineapples or more often stars. The number of points on the stars varied from four to fourteen. I was able to collect a number of the various stone war clubs.

Kamoro lifestyle, markets, problems and needs: the role of carvings

The Kamoro cash economy mostly (but not exclusively) depends on their proximity to markets for their saleable products: fish and mangrove crabs mostly, some sago and a great variety of very occasional hunted or gathered animals: mollusks, monitor lizards, cuscus, cassowaries, wild pigs, turtles. The sale of these products represents the main source of cash for the Kamoro who live near the booming town of Timika. Two much smaller markets for their products are found in the former government and Roman Catholic Church center of Kokonau. In Atuka Village, a long-time Javanese resident and one of his sons formerly bought Kamoro products for resale mostly to Timika. A number of Bugis traders have set up small stores in various Kamoro villages. They purchase items like shark fins and coconuts locally to resell in Timika.

While all the Kamoro now wear western-type clothing, the lifestyle of the majority (except for those living in or near Timika) has changed little from the past. The men fish daily and occasionally hunt, families make sago periodically, the women gather on a daily basis in the mangrove swamps.

A few hundred Kamoro have steady jobs, prestigious work as civil servants (mostly schoolteachers) or are employed with Freeport, while those living near by the government port Pomako find daily jobs as cargo hands. Most of them live in Timika or the town's immediate vicinity. For those Kamoro who have chosen to live in the same area but who do not have a steady job, making

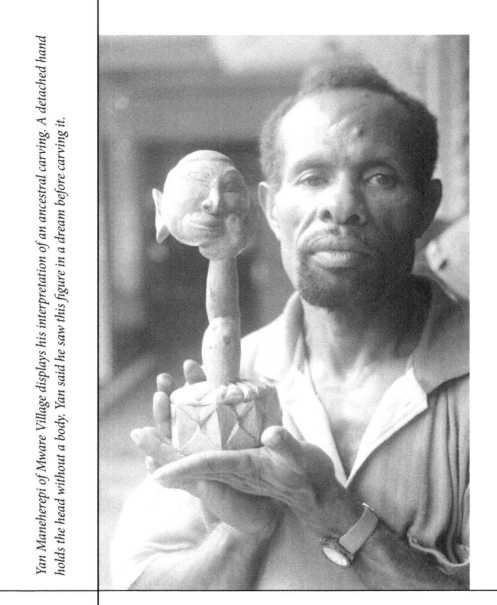

Yan Maneherepi of Mware Village displays his interpretation of an ancestral carving. A detached hand holds the head without a body. Yan said he saw this figure in a dream before carving it.

a living is problematic: they do not have the skills to work in a modern economy and are quite far from their traditional natural resource areas. A fair number have acquired the (devious) skills and connections necessary for taking advantage of various Freeport community programs - or are the direct recipients of a special program to compensate them for a part of their land used by the mining company for their port, road, or tailings deposit area. But many other Kamoro families living near Timika have little opportunity to participate in the cash economy. It is mostly these Kamoro who have taken to make carvings for sale as a source of ready income. All need money for school fees, clothing and daily life essentials such as food, kerosene, collective taxi fares, and modern luxuries like batteries, instant noodles, rice and sugar.

The '*maramowe*': hereditary carvers

In the traditional Kamoro culture, only a few men in each village held the hereditary right to carve. These men were given food and supplies while they carved what was needed for communal rituals, often fulfilling requests by specific families wishing to honor their ancestors. But carving was not a full-time job, and the '*maramowe*' fished, made sago and lived like all the other Kamoro. The term for the carvers comes from '*maramo*' or chisel and '*we*' or person/s.

Today, the '*maramowe*' still dominate the production of some carvings, those made for ritual use. While these men are the creative talent behind the carvings, family members and friends often help them. When a carving is sold, the helpers receive a large part of the payment.

Not all the '*maramowe*' have the necessary talent to produce good carvings. And aside from the basic skills, today's carvings made for sale require the additional factors of imagination and creativity. Some carvers simply try to copy existing designs. Others try to add new shapes and motifs to traditional carvings. And a few try entirely new carving subjects, sometimes inspired by dreams. The time spent in carving varies considerably. This depends mostly on the possibility of sales.

Only one Kamoro carver, Pak Timo Samin, makes his living entirely from carving. Pak Timo and his extended family, some 50 souls, occupy an isolated six-house complex at a crossroads a few kilometers from Timika. Many years ago, Freeport began buying large carvings from Pak Timo and he now has a stream of orders from individuals as well as government personnel, including, occasionally, the military. Several other carvers live in his complex and two of his non-Papuan sons-in-law also participate in the carving process: rough shaping the pieces and the finishing work. Pak Timo is a good businessman, and shows initiative in selling his carvings which have become easier thanks to his reputation. But he has made few carvings that I consider 'artistic' and I have very seldom bought anything from him. Then again, he does not need my business.

An ever-increasing number of men with no hereditary 'rights' to carve do make woodcarvings. Some are quite skilful and have made many sales. There is no resentment against them by the 'maramowe'. Others try but cannot produce good, saleable pieces and give up after several failed attempts and return to fishing and other pursuits.

While some of the cash is undoubtedly wasted on drunkenness and prostitutes, the bulk of it goes to family needs. And the money not only helps the carvers' immediate family but also friends and more distant relatives. It is always heartening to me to see a man, when receiving a good-sized dollop of cash, hand it over to his wife. I know then for sure that it will not be wasted.

The tools of the trade

Before the introduction of metal (perhaps begun by the 1600s but more likely later during the 17th century), we can assume that tough, broken bivalve shells or bones were the 'business ends' of the Kamoro carving tools. The rough shape of the carving was probably hewn out of fairly softwood species with stone axes. These were most likely obtained from the Amungme, located to the north of the Kamoro and living in the highlands where suitable stone blades are found. The Amungme probably traded for these stone axe heads themselves, as most highlands did up to the late 1950s, from a source to the northeast of their homeland, in an area called Yalime. Be that as it may, the trade between the highlands and the lowlands was probably sporadic due to mutual fears of sorcery, along with the high risk of malaria for the Amungme who had ventured outside their high elevation homeland.

While metal itself was imported, iron was worked in Biak and perhaps other areas of the north coast of West New Guinea as well as at Etna Bay, metal tools probably made their way into the western part of Kamoro-land through barter trade with merchants from islands off the south-east coast of Seram Island. 'Massoy' (Cryptocarya massoy) bark (for Javanese folk medicines), birds-of-paradise, 'dammar' pitch and slaves were the products sought by the Muslim traders, in return for metal tools and bits of clothing and cloth for the Kamoro. With metal tools, harder wood and finer designs could then be carved. Metal tools were probably not very widespread in the eastern reaches of Kamoro-land until the early 20th century.

Today, the Kamoro carvers use mostly chisels from Timika, carpenter tools not specifically made for carving. I have distributed sets of finer chisels purchased in Bali to about 80 carvers, and this has had much effect on the details of their sculptures. For most carvings, the general shape is initially made with parangs and axes, with the chisels reserved for more detailed work.

The introduction of metal carving tools has allowed the Kamoro to use more or the denser kinds of wood in their sculptures. Today, many species of trees are used, but a number of carvings are still made with soft, easily worked woods. The problem with these is that, unless very quickly coated with a locally made thick lime wash, they tend to become home to boring insects. These can only be killed by soaking the whole carving in kerosene or placing it in a deep freezer for a couple of weeks. Metal chisels now produce ironwood carvings, near impervious to boring insects.

Kinds of wood used

I have been able to identify only a few of the wood types used today in the Kamoro carvings. I found many Kamoro names for different types of wood used, but we left these out as we were unable to obtain botanical identification for them. In two coastal villages we could only find the scientific names for four species commonly used:

When the proper metal carving tools were available, ironwood, *Intsia bijuga*, 'pota' was often used for their resistance to insects, pleasing color and straight grain.

- *Myristica fatua*, 'pate' - for carving the 'mbitoro'.
- *Sterculia ampala, 'amaata'* - also for 'mbitoro' carvings.
- *Horsfieldia irja*, 'kinakoeke' - for the 'mbitoro' in Kekwa Village (the fruit of this tree is also eaten).
- *Hibiscus tiliaceous, 'iwen'* and *Thespecia populnea, 'doa'* are used for creating drums.

For making canoes and paddles, the harder the wood, the more work but the longer lasting the paddle. Wood types used include *Octomeles sumatrana*, '*yawaro*' and *Capnosperma breviolata,* '*kuku*'. For paddles, *Vatica papuana,* '*pakiro*' was favored in villages by the coast.

Inland carvings included:

- *Hibiscus tiliaceous*, '*iwae*' for making drums; also used: '*peporo*', found only inland. It is said that drums in the west are made from a tree called '*borepa*'.
- *Sterculia ampala*, '*amata*' for the '*mbitoro*' carvings (Iwaka Village); in Pigapu Village, the Kamoro use a tree called '*biro*' as well *Glochidion sp.*

'*Ta'ara*' is a '*dammar*'-like pitch used on the lizard-skin playing surface of drums, heated to tighten the surface to proper tension.

Araucaria cuningamii (?), '*motaro*' called a 'kind of '*dammar*', used in Pigapu for the same purpose as above: tightening the playing surface of drums.

In Iwaka, the wood of the '*aotao*', '*koa*' and the '*opadomupao*' trees are also used for making the body of the drums.

Trumpets are made of a kind of bamboo called '*mbiti*'.

There seems to be little overlap with Papua New Guinea. The Encyclopedia of Papua New Guinea tells us that *Alstonia scholaris* is used to carve bowls; for durable carving to sell to tourists they use *Intsia bijuga* and *Pterocarpus indicus,* with the occasional use of *Vitex cofassus*. Hourglass-type drums (hand-held and covered with lizard or snake skin) are made from the rosewood *Pterocarpus indicus* while the large, upright slit gongs, on the Sepik and the Ramu Rivers from *Vitex cofassus*. Pajimans mentions *Albizia* spp. as a wood often used for carving.

Spirited participants arrive in their canoes from different villages, later used for races. During the last festivities, over 3,000 Kamoro participated in the yearly Kamoro Kakuru festival.

THE YEARLY KAMORO KAKURU FESTIVALS

10

Wearing a spirit mask, a performer dances in the competition along with others from his village. The event proved too hard to judge and finally each dance team received the same amount of money for their participation.

(Note: for a somewhat different description of the festivals, in many areas more complete than mine, see Jacobs 2011.)

The Kamoro Kakuru festival began a revival of Kamoro art. This festival was originally inspired by the yearly Asmat auction of carvings, but from the beginning it was considerably larger and more elaborate. While a crucial aspect of the Kamoro Kakuru was the auction and sales of carvings, there were a number of other events such as traditional dancing, and canoe racing. Temporary housing, various facilities such as toilets, a health clinic and food were also provided for the participants.

For a number of years, Freeport had supported the Asmat festival where I was one of the judges in the group that chose the best carvings in various categories. During one of these Asmat festivals, in 1996, I asked Paul Murphy, a senior Freeport vice-president, why the company did not sponsor such a festival for the Kamoro. Several Kamoro villages had traditional land rights in the areas used by the mining company for its port and other infrastructure, as well as the river and large plot of land where the mill's wastes (tailings) were deposited.

On the spot, Mr. Murphy agreed. What's more, he put me in charge of organizing a yearly festival for the Kamoro as soon as possible. That was a bit more than I had bargained for, but with a great deal of help from Freeport, I started. In order to familiarize the Kamoro with a large-scale cultural event and art auction, I took a group of 15 carvers and leaders to Agats to attend the yearly Asmat event in 1997. We traveled there in a large dugout canoe with an outboard motor. The journey took 36 hours, which included spending a night bobbing around thank-God calm seas. Our boatman missed the turnoff from the open water to the channel-estuary leading to Agats, due to smoke from an El Niño event. It was not the most comfortable night of our lives, but we survived in relatively good spirits. The Asmat festival was an eye-opener for the Kamoro.

The Kamoro carvers had the opportunity to meet with and exchange ideas with their Asmat counterparts. They saw the carvings that had been produced for the festival. While the carving techniques are quite similar, the styles and designs are markedly different - to a practiced eye. But the auction really rocked the Kamoro back on their heels: the noise, the excitement and, perhaps most of all, the high prices paid for many of the carvings, much more than the Kamoro had ever received for any of their sculptures. Of course, they wanted a festival of their own.

When we returned to Timika, it was up to me to organize a similar show. Where to start? First, I formed a small committee of a dozen or so Kamoro leaders and carvers to work out the various items in the organization of the festival. We held regular meetings, sometimes with a government or Freeport staff. The Kamoro on the committee received a small stipend.

Our first concerns were: where to hold the festival? How many Kamoro to invite? Then what events should we hold? How to house and feed the participants? What infrastructure would we need? How much money to allocate to each aspect of the festival? I wanted to show the most characteristic and unique features of the Kamoro culture, and sought to make a show attractive to both the Kamoro as well as to visitors. And we wanted to give the Kamoro a venue to help restore and foster pride in their traditional culture. With this in mind, we put an emphasis on carvings for display and sale, with an auction to try to bring the highest prices for individual carvers. Along with this, we organized canoe races and a dance competition among the villages.

Before any other business, we had to find a location for the festival. With a number of the Kamoro leaders and elders, we selected an area near in Hiripau Village where an area between the main road from Timika to the south, and a bend of the Wania River was large enough for our needs. There was enough space (after clearing many trees and thick vegetation) for building a large hall for dancing, opening ceremonies, art displays and the auction. Outside of this hall, we needed a large area cleared for some open space and simple raised shelters for the participants. The Wania River there was wide enough for canoe races as well as having plenty of 'parking spaces' for the dozens and dozens of dugout canoes which were to bring the participants. The area was also chosen as it was next to a decent road running 27 kilometers from Timika for easy access to visitors.

Our next steps included fixing a date for the festival and deciding on how many Kamoro to invite to participate from each village or settlement. Each group was to be provided with basic accommodations (a hut with a raised floor and a thatch roof), toilet facilities along with meals and drinking water, plus a stipend for petrol for their outboard engines.

Freeport's contributions

The Kamoro festival could never have been held without a great deal of cash contribution from Freeport. Aside from financing the total budget necessary, the company helped in many different ways. Most of the guests at the festival, foreign and Indonesian, were either Freeport staff, employees or company guests. These invitees were the crucial actors who made the auction of carvings a success, bidding up the pieces to high levels – to the joy of the individual carvers who had never seen such sky-high prices for their work. And thanks to the number of Freeport employees and guests, no piece was left unsold at any of the auctions. The company also provided for free shipping of any carvings bought at the festival from Timika to Jakarta.

During the first couple of festivals, the local government gave us considerable help. The '*bupati*' (the chief government official of our district) himself a Kamoro, frequently called meetings of officials to promote the festival and help with its organization. Later on, with another '*bupati*', this help was considerably reduced. By then, Freeport had delegated some more of its staff to help organize several key aspects of the festival. Every year, a company team, used to working on waterways, efficiently arranged the canoe races. Freeport drivers shuttled staff and guests back and forth between the festival site and their accommodations at the company-owned hotel in Timika. Medical staff from Freeport attended to all the participants, (and any other Papuan) needing health-related attention.

Freeport made special payments to the military and the police to provide security. During the first festival, there were unfortunately too many soldiers strutting around with automatic weapons, creating the impression that there was danger in the air. Subsequently, weapons were concealed and the military presence was much more subtle, as per the company's (and my) request.

Out to the villages: spreading the news

While I could reach a few Kamoro settlements by road from Timika, for most of the villages is was only by water. I canoed with a couple of Kamoro friends to announce the date of the upcoming festival and explain the various rules and regulations such as the number of participants from each village, the various events, and how many carvings to bring. From past stays in various villages, I knew that it was close to impossible to hold a meeting anytime but at night: men and women are busy fishing, foraging, and collecting in the day. Daytime finds only small children and old folks in most villages. So it's spending the night in each village if one wants to get any information across. This way, we extended invitations to some 40 Kamoro villages and six Sempan ones.

We brought along coffee, sugar and cigarettes, the three essentials for any Kamoro meeting, doubly ensuring an audience. Having a European spend the night in the village was an initial draw. It was only very occasionally in the past that a Dutch priest would spend time in a settlement, and some villages never had hosted a 'white man' overnight.

The canoe races and dancing were relatively easy to explain. But the central focus of the festival, the art auction, was more difficult. Fortunately, we had taken with us a man who had seen the Asmat auction, so he could put things more clearly, from their perspective. I knew enough about Kamoro carvings (see the previous chapter) to have devised several major categories for prizes. Some were similar to those of the Asmat, but there were others as the two groups have different subject matter as well as different styles. The Kamoro had no Asmat 'story-board' or scenes of daily life categories. Both groups carve tall totem-pole-like sculptures used ritually to represent ancestors and both also carve hollowed out hourglass-shaped drums. While the Asmat carve 'normal' shields with cultural-based motifs identifying major art-producing areas, the Kamoro shields are highly stylized and come in a bewildering array of shapes and styles; most of them would not be of any use in real tribal warfare.

Other Kamoro carvings 'categories' included hollow ancestral figures, walking sticks and sago bowls. While there had been few if any carvings of animals, I decided to add this subject, along with a 'free creation' '*kreasi bebas*' section. Later, animals and free creation were combined. Two more categories were added in later years, as part of a drive to preserve items of cultural value in danger of extinction. Spirit masks were very seldom used in any ceremonies today (I had only seen them used twice) and only very old men knew how to make these. So we inserted a 'spirit mask' category, with these large items made either of strips of palm leaves, sheets of bark or plaited rattan.

As the art of carving canoes was also falling into disuse, we started giving prizes for the best ones. I'm sorry to report that this did not result in much of a canoe-carving revival. In the old days, many canoes bore fairly elaborate carvings, almost all of open fretwork, and not part of the structure of the boat but made separately and mounted on the prow, apparently for festive occasions. Canoes submitted for prizes at the festival showed ancestral figures in the bow (male) and stern (female) whose purpose was to protect the canoe's occupants. A number of canoes showed a thin strip of geometric-like carvings along the upper and outer sides of the canoe, representing the craft's use in fishing. Thus these stylized motifs included items such as fish scales and fins, and shark's teeth. Over the years, with the arrival of the modern world, these carved canoes slowly disappeared as the dugouts became strictly utilitarian. Through prize money given to canoes during the yearly Kamoro festival, carvings on them began to reappear. Unfortunately, this stopped when the yearly festivals were no longer held. Later, only the odd model-sized canoe with carvings was made for exhibition and sale.

Due to men's (worldwide) propensity to spend money foolishly, I tried to think of events to put money directly into the Kamoro ladies' pockets. Success in this endeavor has been quite limited so far. The women plaited strips of vegetal fibers into shoulder bags and items of clothing, but none particularly were well made and we have had problems selling them at the Kamoro festival and elsewhere. For the past several years, my wife Jina worked with several groups of ladies in an attempt to improve the quality of the plaitings. But sales were still discouragingly few. If the marketing of these women's crafts have been less than unsuccessful, the ladies canoe races have been the surprise hit of the various Kamoro festivals. Initially, we only had men's canoe races, of two types: standing and sitting while paddling, as this reflects the normal way to paddle in the eastern and western areas of Kamoro-land respectively. After the third year of the festival, we added the ladies' canoe races to be able to give the prize money directly to the women. This event became a top draw in the festival, generating the most enthusiastic support, shouts and excitement of any event. The auction of carvings could bring in much more money, but, except for the carver and his relatives, the level of tangible excitement was nowhere near that of the ladies' canoe races.

The festival's changing locations

While the first Kamoro Kakuru (23-27 April 1998) was a success from most points of view, a serious problem developed. Shortly before the opening of the festival, some of the Kamoro groups felt slighted in the locations of the temporary huts put up for them as well as feeling that they had not received their fair share of food. A mini-riot ensued but was stopped before it got out of hand. A meeting was held where the grievances were addressed. It was agreed to proceed with the festival after it had been almost cancelled.

A very positive element for the revival of the Kamoro culture first appeared in the 1998 festival. Our dance competition re-enacted oral traditions, including the use of the mask where needed in legends shown in dances. We had some major problems with judging the dance completion, so changes were made to satisfy the participants as well as the appreciative Kamoro audience.

Due to some long-standing unresolved problems and jealousy between Hiripau and some other villages, it was decided not to hold the festival at that location the following year. The political circumstances of the country in 1999, especially the strict security measures for the presidential elections, mandated a much smaller festival that year. The government and the military told us to hold the festival in the town of Timika.

While much fewer participants and carvers showed up in 1999, the quality of the sculptures had improved considerably, thanks to the stimulus provided by the previous year's auction and the concomitant appreciation of the art by the outside world. There was a sense of re-awakening among the Kamoro artists but they were still far from achieving the quality and the imagination of their forefathers' carvings on display in several European museums. But it was hoped that the festival, then scheduled to become a yearly event in mid-October, would keep stimulating the long dormant talents of the Kamoro artists. We decided that any outsider interested was welcomed just by showing up at the festival. While it was not held specially for tourists, we would gladly admit any visitors interested in this fascinating culture. However, only foreign and Indonesian guests were brought to Timika by Freeport, flown from Jakarta and housed in the four-star company-owned hotel. We only had a couple of art dealers who came by paying their way to Timika.

For the following year, 2000, we chose Pigapu Village for the festival as the best possible location. It was on the Wania River, with plenty of 'parking space' for the canoes of the participants, plus a long straight stretch of water for the races. Pigapu Village had recently moved back to their old site, located at the end of a very rough logging road to Wania River called 'lopon' (for log pond) where the cut trees were loaded for shipment to the sea. The area was 47 kilometers southwest from Timika on a road [There was also a road to the village, not in very good condition,] barely passable, especially after a heavy rain. I contacted the head offices of two companies working with Freeport on the company's infrastructure – GSBJ and Petrosea – for help to improve the road. This road was to cause lots of headaches in the following years, but a number of participants lived inland and the road was the only access for them. It was also the only practical means of access to the festival grounds for Freeport employees, guests, and government officials.

The festival in 2000 was held from 12 to 15 October. My wife and I spent over a month there to supervise the various infrastructure works necessary for the festival. At first, we stayed with a Kamoro friend in a tiny room, then in a mini-house built specially for us, but with no running water or real toilet.

For the festivals, the men of Pigapu built a U-shaped walkway lined with simple huts for each village of participants. They were provided with firewood and mats made by the local ladies. A dock was erected on the river for washing and a row of toilets made on stilts over the river. A '*jalan tikus*' or footpath along the river was cleared so that people could gather to watch the canoe races and also find access to the river to their boats. For their work, we paid a stipend to all the residents of Pigapu. A large, raised open hall was constructed of hardwood for the auction by Freeport contractors who also built a clinic at the top of the village so that participants could get a health check during the festival from the Malaria Control Unit .

Apollo Takati, a good friend, headed the organizing committee. We worked well together and I was able to concentrate on the carvings selection and auction, especially after having seen to the festival infrastructure, especially paving of the road.

Problems

During the first three years when we held the festival at Pigapu, we had to resolve several major problems. One was a mini-riot in 2000 when one particular village's dance group felt that they should have won the top prize. There was also unhappiness among the losers of the ladies '*anyaman*' contest. They felt that it was unfair that such large sums of money (Rp 1.5, 1 and 0.5 million) were given to the top three winners while the other participants who had put in lots of hard work got nothing. We decided that from year 2002 onwards, there would be no prizes. Each village that presented a dance or ladies '*anyaman*' would receive a fixed amount of money that was divided among them from the pot.

Drinking water for the participants was another problem. At great expense to Freeport, a huge drill rig was brought to Pigapu to attempt to reach an underground freshwater source. The drill reached a bit over 100 meters, but the clean groundwater table was not reached. So we had to truck in drinking water that would not always arrive on time and in sufficient quantities. A riot was narrowly averted when no drinking water arrived one morning... but two water trucks eventually showed up, to my great relief.

While alcohol was forbidden at the festival, supplies somehow sneaked in. The Kamoro seem to favor binge drinking, leading to expected results: drunks making a nuisance of themselves. We had Indonesian police (both Papuan and non-Papuan) at the festival grounds and they came up with an excellent solution. Instead of arresting the drunks, the police simply forced them to sit in the river until the alcohol's effects wore off.

The timing of the festival created problems as well. The months of April and October are generally the ones with the calmest seas. The Kamoro villages located in the west had no choice but to arrive at least part of the way by sea and the waves can become dangerously rough at times. Starting in the central Kamoro area, there are interconnected estuaries and other waterways where canoe travel is safe, as they are protected from heavy seas. However, using the seas for motorized canoe travel is faster but uses expensive fuel. We had hoped to establish the Kamoro festival at the same time each year, following the practice of the Asmat one, held in October every year. This was so that visitors could plan their visits to the Kamoro festival long ahead of time. However, due to various circumstances, we had to switch back and forth between April and October, so there was no long-range planning possible for potential foreign or Indonesian guests.

The festival rules allowed for 20 participants from each village. These were to be provided with shelter and food for five days. However, some villages came with well over 20 persons and many non-participants also showed up. And everyone expected to be provided with housing and food. While the total number of participants in the budget was around 800, at the last festival in 2006 some 3,000 plus showed up, all clamoring for food and shelter. Reminding them of the 20-per-village rule did not help a whit. All Kamoro felt they had the 'right' to participate and thus receive shelter and food for the five-day duration. Perhaps we should have followed the rules of attendance at the yearly Asmat festival. Each participant had to find his own way to Agats, the festival location, and take care of his own meals and accommodation.

The following festivals

After a mini-riot by one village unhappy about not winning in the 2000 dance competition, the committee decided to take all rules off the dances presented at the festival. These could last as long as the performers wished, and each group could field as many dancers as they wanted. One village group, from Kaugapu, presented the 'ant dance', with over 40 performers with some clambering up vines (like ants) to specially built tower. The group told the committee they wanted to present a dance that showed how Kamoro people would work together. (Jacobs, 2011)

Starting in 2001, we tried to help more Kamoro women so they could receive financial benefits. Starting canoe races that year was a huge success in terms of popularity with the Papuan audience, and of course the prize money for the winners – the same as for the men's races – went directly to the ladies.

The Kamoro themselves took the initiative for activities that had not been planned by the organizing committee. When a group of canoes arrived together from different villages, they landed amidst shouts and high enthusiasm to join with their paddles in a huge circle dance. During the second festival in Pigapu, a group of Kamoro, on their own initiative, made a *'mbitoro'* that was erected in front of the auction hall. This marked an invitation to participate by their ancestors. At night, some elders from various villages joined in a *'mbake'*, continuous singing and drumming to invite the ancestors, that lasted nearly to dawn. (Jacobs, 2011). Also at night, young men and women were drawn to the *'seka'*, a contemporary dance popular in West New Guinea.

From 2000 onwards, the Kamoro participants themselves organized an *'oo'kame'* the ceremonial killing of several pigs to conclude the festival.

After a few festivals, the organizing committee became more involved, allowing me time for the village visits to announce the festivals and to concentrate on the carvings and the auction. Sections of the committee were delegated for various specific tasks, such as security, the dance competition, canoe races, building of the shelters and food provision. Freeport staff gradually participated less in the organization of the festival (although it covered all the expenses) while the committee was taken over by members of LEMASKO, a Kamoro foundation (also financed by Freeport). The organizing committee expanded to 87 members by 2005.

As the festival attracted more and more attention, the local government took an increased interest. In 2001, the festival was officially opened with

Each year, a number of carvings are selected from each village for sale at the festival auction. One item reached the sale price of $1,100 but that was most unusual. Most pieces went for $200-$400.

a speech by the '*bupati*' (regent) an ethnic Kamoro. This was followed by speeches by other local government worthies. The following year, the local government financed the building of a house for the members of the organizing committee that wanted to sleep at the festival site instead of returning to their homes around Timika every night. That year, the vice-'*bupati*', also an ethnic Kamoro, officially presented the equivalent of some $10,000 to the organizing committee. The sum vanished quickly from view. The following year, the government tourist office gave about $20,000 in cash to the organizing committee which also disappeared. In 2005, the province's governor, Jaap Salossa opened the festival with a 'gift' of $30,000. It quickly went missing as well. This sum also went astray from any official financial account of the festival. For a few corrupt Kamoro, the festival was a personal financial treasure trove. No one from the government ever advised the committee about any financial aid ahead of time so the sum could be allocated officially to the festival expenses.

The auctions

The festival auctions were the opposite of the staid bidding at Sotherby's or Christie's. Ours were raucous affairs, with lots of shouting, laughter and good-natured (usually) challenges among buyers who often knew each other. Carvers, whose figures had been selected, were allowed in the auction hall with all other festival participants crowding around the sides trying to see what was happening inside.

Based partially on my work as one of the judges at the Asmat art festival, I divided the carvings into a number of similar categories. But I also expanded the 'free creation' category that now included items like a chessboard with Kamoro-like figures, miniature canoes and bookshelves with '*wemawe*' as bookends. For picking the auction carvings, we made up a small group, including two Kamoro, to help in the selection, including Dirk Smidt of the Leiden Museum when he was in attendance. The final choice was usually mine, as the carvers knew that I was completely neutral in my picks. It would have been impossible to ask the Kamoro to select the carvings, as they would have been accused of favoritism toward their friends. When each selection was made, we took Polaroid and color photos of each object which was tagged with the names of the carver, his village as well as its category. I tried to select at least one carving from every village even, if the quality was not among

Our spirited auctioneer, Apollo Takati, dances and shouts enthusiastically to raise the bids at the auction. Usually a staid official, Pak Apollo's personality changes for the event.

THE YEARLY KAMORO KAKURU FESTIVALS 131

the best. The buyers received the Polaroid photo for identification purposes. Carvers carefully noted what was picked for their future work, adapting themselves to the market. After a three-dimensional figure sold well one year, several appeared in subsequent auctions. (Jacobs, 2011). (For more on the selection of carving, see the next chapter.)

Before the auction began, all the carvings that had been picked were lined up on the stage. Buyers were invited to browse to whet their appetite for any special item that caught their fancy. My wife and I were on the stage to explain carvings to anyone interested. We were both dressed as traditional Kamoro (with a few modifications) to show that we were not ashamed of wearing this clothing and to underline our solidarity with this group. I opened the auction with a short talk and introduced our Kamoro auctioneer. During our first festival in 1998, I had asked Juven Biakai, the Asmat auctioneer (and head of the Asmat Museum) to handle the bidding, but switched to Kamoro men for subsequent festivals. They spoke some English but the auction was conducted in Indonesian while I translated for the foreign buyers.

I started off by selecting an item and inviting its carver to come up on the stage. Several men started drumming on the stage as the carver, the auctioneer and myself danced and shouted to create a fevered ambiance.

Soon the carver was joined by his helpers and family, all-dancing with the selected item. The auctioneer then shouted a low price in Indonesian and I translated. As the price kept rising, the dancing became more frenetic. Sometimes when a very high bid was reached, a bedlam of shouts and drumming reached a crescendo as the final bid was reached. The buyer came on stage to pay and receive his prize. The carver was paid immediately. And on to the next item. Often, I had to hurry the bidding as the time for the auction on two successive days was limited and I did not want any items to remain unsold. At every auction we would sell about 140 pieces in total.

The highest price reached during the auctions was the equivalent of $1,100 for a beautiful sailfish, by Ricardus Nimi. Curious as to how he spent his windfall, I interviewed him: he said he divided all the money among his assistants and relatives, keeping only $50 for himself. Other carvers told me they had made similar divisions. Some guests bought large carvings thanks to Freeport shipping the items to Jakarta. But the next most expensive auction carving was a small one, a 'wemawe mbiikao' sold for $980. Carving is the exclusive preserve of men, so we were surprised when a woman presented an excellent sago bowl. I hyped up this item in the auction, backing the putative lady carver. The bowl sold for a higher

Foreign art dealers and collectors, as well as Freeport staff bid on the carvings selected for the auction. Competition between bidders was quite keen, raising high prices for the carvers.

price than any of these items made by a man. But later I found out that her husband had made it. Much of the money from the auction ended up in Timika shops for food to take home, along with household items. Some of the funds ended up for school fees, and as partial payments for outboard motors. While no subsequent carvings reached $1,100, in general, the prices increased every year.

The possibility of making money from carvings was not lost on the young Kamoro men. During the festivals, and later in the villages, I saw a number of talented men in their 20s making excellent carvings. Karen Jacobs wrote that the festivals led to an increase in the carvings' cultural esteem both locally and internationally. (Jacobs, 2011)

Positive aspects of the festival

In spite of a number of problems, the festivals' effects were quite positive for the Kamoro. There had never been such a large gathering, with all villages represented. This gave a unique opportunity for the Kamoro to get to know their fellows from far-away villages with no previous communications between them. The festival gave a chance for long-separated friends and relatives to meet again. I had hoped that the occasion of so many representative groups from the various villages would result in some form of Kamoro-wide solidarity. Although this happened to a certain extent, the inter-village meetings did not translate into some sort of political movement that could take advantage of the numbers of Kamoro. There are more Kamoro in the Mimika district than any other single linguistic group, so if they could have spoken with one voice their concerns would carry more weight with the local and national politicians.

During the nights, there was spontaneous dancing, sometimes by a single village, other times with young people from many villages joining in a popular introduced dance with courtship opportunities. Older people from various villages socialized with their fellows by night-time fires, talking for hours and hours.

During the various dances performed by each village, a great deal of pride was in evidence. Perhaps more important than the admiration of outsiders, the performers were proud to show their dances to their fellow Kamoro. This applied to the canoe races as well, another opportunity to show off strength in skills and coordination.

Paulus Amareyau with his carving of a preying mantis. The carving was sold at the auction in the 'free creation' category for a high price.

The quality of Kamoro art took a huge leap thanks to a yearly festival that ran from 1998 to 2006. For this festival, with the Asmat one as only a very general model, I defined various traditional categories and gave out three cash prizes in each one. These prizes and the possibility of their carvings being selected for the festival's auctions greatly encouraged the Kamoro to carve fine pieces again. There is no question that the trend is toward a degree of commercialism, but that is not necessarily bad. And my choices of course affected the pieces produced. There are no more ancient Kamoro carvings. On the other hand, there are a few serious collectors and many buyers who just want an attractive piece. The Kamoro men need cash. Making carvings for sale may not be ideal according to purists, but this makes sense in today's situation in the Kamoro/modern world context. Western artists certainly hope that their paintings will sell!

Of course, from a financial point of view, the carvers were the happiest lot, with good prices paid for their work even outside the auction. The festival provided them with an unheard-of large market and the opportunity to show off their carving skills in front of their fellow Kamoro as well as the visitors. The carvers displayed any pieces not selected for the auction on the raised walkway outside their accommodations. Visitors to the festival walked around on the walkways, checking out the carvings and purchased some right away. The buyers had to bargain in Indonesian or by sign language. Many items were sold this way but we had some problems as some of the carvers expected the organizing committee to buy any and all unsold pieces. We did buy some of the unsold items at a low price of some $5. But there were just too many to purchase and this caused some resentment.

One of the main reasons for holding the festival was to cultivate the carving tradition that was on its way to disappearing, so the traditional woodcarving skills would not be lost forever. In this, the festival at least partially fulfilled its purpose.

Freeport also received a considerable amount of sorely needed positive publicity thanks to the festival. The company has come under endless negative censure for its environmental and human rights policies. Ambassadors and high central government officials invited by Freeport to the festival were given tours of the mine and shown the company's programs to mitigate the damage to the environment and to alleviate ongoing human rights abuses, some by Freeport security personnel (but mostly by the Indonesian military). The visit by a national ex-minister of Education resulted in the building of a school in Pigapu. The guests also saw the clinic Freeport had built in Pigapu, initially for the festival but staffed at other times for a few years.

The bottom line: why the festival was cancelled

Freeport asked me to be in charge when the festivals began. I took control of all aspects, helped by a Kamoro organizing committee. How well this system worked can certainly be questioned, but I feel that by and large it worked well enough initially under the circumstances. Our organization continued until the 2003 festival when Freeport decided that the Kamoro should run the festival themselves. I remained in charge of the carvings selection and the auction, as it was difficult for any Kamoro to be objective in picking the pieces. But the Freeport decision meant that the festival's finances passed into the hands of an organizing committee.

While some members of the organizing committee were honest, others were less so. Perhaps they felt that as Freeport was paying, the cost did not matter. Contracts were given out to friends for items like the necessary road improvement and bridge building, with kickbacks leading to unreasonably expensive levels. The food section of the committee charged far above budget. The fuel section of the committee was supposed to take enough petrol for the canoe outboards for the round-trip to the festival. Some villages received no fuel at all, or in lesser quantities than required. But the funds allocated for fuel were always fully 'spent', in other words, some of the money 'disappeared'.

A contract given out by one of the committee sections in 2004 for building toilets for the festival came in with a bill for an extortionary amount of money where 150 classy hardwood toilets where built when 70 with local materials would have sufficed. There were no funds in the budget to pay for this, especially at the price asked. But the Kamoro involved in the scam insisted on payment and blocked the road leading to Pigapu to stop everyone from coming by land. Some of the villages coming by canoe had already arrived. Arguments flew back and forth between the Kamoro and violence was threatening. We decided the best course of action was to cancel the festival for that year.

The amount of funds needed for the festival thus ballooned beyond reason. Freeport's total financial outlay in 2006 was five to six times the first year's budget. Even after the festival was over, contractors and committee section heads demanded more money from the company. This amounted to a total of well over $300,000. That was when Freeport decided to 'pull the plug'. No more festivals. While the company was ready to contribute to the festival's expenses, it no was longer ready to finance limitless budgets. The company requested that the government organize and lead the festivals. Unfortunately, for the Kamoro culture, this never happened. I have met with some of the highest local officials and they all thought that the festival should continue. But they never followed this up in practice.

In order to keep the carving tradition alive, I started a Freeport-funded program where I personally went to Kamoro villages to purchase carvings. (See the next chapter)

Often Kamoro carvers came to where I was living in Timika to sell me one or more pieces. I bought only a few of these, as the gallery I ran was usually well stocked. The carvers would then sell their items to one of several souvenir shops that operated close together on one of Timika's main streets. Of course, these shops would pay a very low price but at least the carver did not have to return home without any money. The Bugis-run souvenir shops were our main competitors in town. They specialized in the most common Papuan souvenirs, such as the highlands penis sheaths, often over decorated with fanciful, non-traditional designs. We kept to better quality genuine art items.

The carver Ponsius Amini of Mware Village produced this strange carving combining his carving skills with far-out imagination. All his carvings sold the minute they went on sale.

11 PICKING AND INFLUENCING KAMORO ART

The exquisitely proportioned masked figure has only his arms and legs showing. It represents a spirit. The elegant carving shows an aspect of true Kamoro art.

The supply of fine old carvings, shining with patina from wear, produced by traditional societies has dwindled to almost nothing at the present. A long-kept heirloom piece occasionally gets sold for financial reasons, but very few are left in the hands of their indigenous owners. Over the past decades, the number of old pieces coming onto the market from tribal cultures have dwindled. Ancient carvings command sky-high prices. Most of the old tribal carvings now bought and sold come from collectors, not from the areas of their (former) production.

However, this lack of supply of old carvings does not mean the demise of tribal carvings. Some groups still produce traditional carvings for their own ritual or practical use. There are also many carvings produced for sale only. The quality of these commercial pieces varies tremendously, from the 'firewood' category, to that of fine, modern art. While some of the carvings still fulfill a role in the traditional religion, others are made for sale. The eminent New York art critic Clement Greenberg wrote that modern paintings, having ceased to be illustrative, ought to be decorative.

A few drums were the only (relatively) ancient pieces I've seen among the Kamoro. These were perhaps up to 40-odd years old. Drums are sometimes kept as heirlooms and passed down from one generation to the next. The drums are kept over fires or hung inside the huts, and so can be preserved far longer than the other carvings that quickly deteriorate outside in the hot, humid climate with hordes of wood-boring insects. In the past, the '*mbitoro*' were taken to the sago fields after their ritual use had been finished. This was to ensure good sago harvests, thanks to the intervention of the ancestors. The practice stopped sometime in the past. Now, after the '*karapao*' initiation ritual, the '*mbitoro*' is left to rot in place. Unless I purchase it. I'm aware of only one occasion when the '*mbitoro*' was broken up and the pieces taken home by the families of the important men represented therein. These families had paid and/or fed the carvers that had worked on the '*mbitoro*', the usual practice.

For nearly 20 years, during the yearly Kamoro festival (1998-2005) and afterwards, I purchased carvings (and a few other items) from the various villages of this artistic group. I later staged exhibits, thanks to Freeport logistical help, during which the carvings were sold.

Urbanus Emaru of Wonosari Jaya Village combined human arms and hands with a turtle body. The composite animal displays typical abstract motifs. A real turtle shell covers the back of the carving.

What were my qualifications for such a job? As a young man, during the early 1960s, I 'dealt' fairly successfully in African carvings. Later in life, I bought and sold tribal art from Vanuatu (then called New Hebrides) for fun and profit. The bulk of the African carvings I dealt with were quite old and of very high monetary value. But I bought and sold some contemporary pieces as well. In Vanuatu, after buying a carving or a clay-modeled item at the agreed price, I returned to the seller and gave him a part of my profits, to everyone's amazement. But while I did this partially to assuage my conscience at my ridiculously high profit margins, there was another benefit: I built up enough trust that many previously fine hidden pieces (some quite old!) were brought out for sale to me during my return trips.

I collected a few pieces for a hoped-for potential museum in Timika, but the bulk of my festival selection and subsequent purchases had to please whoever wanted to buy them. My storage space was limited, and this restricted the number of carvings I could hold in stock. I was 'stuck' with any carvings I cannot sell. So, a prime criterion was: will the piece sell?

Criteria for Kamoro art purchases

My criteria in picking Kamoro art combine creativity and aesthetics, both within the defined categories of their art (such as stylized shields, drum handles, ancestor figures, sago bowls) as well as 'new art' pieces, such as fantastical animals (sometimes combining animal bodies with human limbs). Creativity and aesthetics are difficult words to define, and, as we all know, beauty is in the eyes of the beholder. But, another truism says that the eye sees what it is trained to see. And the rational mind, with some experience, calculates what can sell.

Defining artistic criteria is not an easy task for me, having had no formal training and little contact with the world of art criticism. As everyone else, I too initially react to a carving from what seems like an instinctive like or dislike. Of course, the 'instinctive' part of our criteria has been shaped by the culture(s) to which we have been exposed. When, upon due reflection, defining words do spill out, they are vague: harmony, expression, proportions, and shapes, the flow of a carving, color combinations, and the wood's hue. Simple lines making for powerful pieces characterize much of the best of traditional tribal art.

A large ancestor carving made of ironwood and weighing over 200 kilograms. It was carved by Nikodemus Kaumakopeyau of Mioko Village. It was difficult to sell but eventually brought some $400 to Pak Nikodemus.

There may be some so-called 'objective' criteria, such as the expressiveness of a face with knitted brows implying concentration, intensity, or anger. This way of reacting might apply to outsiders, if not necessarily to the Kamoro. The stylistic device, the knitted brow, is quite common on most ancestor carvings (called '*wemawe*') but carvers only say that the 'knitted brows' is the way they learned to carve these sculptures and cannot elaborate any further. The same holds true of several carvers who extend the lower face and chin into an outward curve, resembling that of large spirit masks. None have been able to verbalize any reason for doing this. Indeed, while most carvers very willingly go into lengthy and elaborate explanations as to the mythological content of their carvings, they only say 'this is the way we have always done it' when asked about any stylistic features. Or that the carving initiated from one seen in a dream.

Looking at a carving with a critical eye, I try to 'judge' it first and foremost by an instinctive response to it, then with a more objective appraisal. How well are the various elements of the carving integrated into the overall piece? Do the human or spirit faces show any expression? How well are the bodies, human and animal, rendered? Here we often have unusual shapes, limbs or features intentionally out of proportion blending wondrously (or not) into the overall carving. A head and arms might be far from the legs and feet, with a connecting torso blended into the fretwork at the center of the carving. Indeed, any human (or other) subject begun at the top of a stylized shield ('*yamate*') might wander through the solid or open fretwork of the central portion to re-emerge at the lower end. How obviously or subtlety is this rendered? This definitely, is another of my criteria.

Aside from the creativity in the traditional Kamoro categories, I also looked for this feature in unusual subject matter in a section that I have called 'free creation'. Often these are phantasmagorical animals sometimes blend human features such as in the hands and feet, and, very occasionally, the face. There are a limited number of animals (mostly cassowaries and hornbills) in the traditional art that have been collected in the past. In these animals, the natural proportions of the various body parts are almost always respected. In the 'free creations', other animals appear: insects (the preying mantis, grasshoppers), crustaceans (shrimp, crabs) fish, sharks, stingrays, turtles and crocodiles, or a very occasional dog, a pig or tree kangaroo.

Niko Ukapoka of Kamoro Jaya Village specialized in a large fish with a hollow body that served as a traditional bowl under a well-fitted lid. He made many similar colorful containers but could not carve and paint enough to keep up with the demand. Freeport expat staff wives lined up to order his fish carvings.

Resurrection and new creation

Thanks to the Kooijman book, we were able to 'resurrect' some items of Kamoro art. These include large and elaborate spirit masks, ('*mbiikao*') usually made either from bark and rattan. I saw one of these masks used in only one village (Iwaka), surfacing during a boys' initiation ritual. The usual rituals associated elsewhere with these masks, with only a single exception, seemed to have died out, but some older men still knew how to make them. Thanks to the creation of a 'spirit mask' category at the yearly Kamoro festival, some of the elders taught young men how to make these masks and they had begun appearing in several villages - although never in the old funerary rituals formerly associated with them.

In the old days, many canoes bore fairly elaborate carvings, almost all of open fretwork, and, according to Kooijman, 'not part of the structure of the boat but made separately and mounted on the prow, apparently for festive occasions'. The yearly Kamoro festival partially resurrected the art of carving canoes but after the demise of the Kamoro Kakuru this stopped. Normal canoes with (or without) carvings are too heavy and bulky for purchase (and shipping) so no clients were interested. Instead, 'model' mini canoes were made with decorative carvings, some quite artistic, holding inside human figures and an occasional dog. These were popular and relatively easy to sell.

The types of carvings found in Kooijman (thus mostly collected prior to the 1960s) and still being produced, include the '*mbitoro*', '*wemawe*', an occasional crucifix or crucifix/'*mbitoro*' combination. Other kinds of old-style carvings include animals (hornbills and cassowaries), drums, and a variety of types of '*yamate*' (solid and 'open'). Everyday items still carved include sago bowls, paddles, sago beaters, carving tools, a very occasional unadorned spear (but no arrowheads such as those illustrated), a few war clubs (the old stones re-bound onto a new shaft), no neck rests, but some combs, lots of plaited fiber bags and (occasionally) various personal ornaments.

Items out of the blue included the type of large chest pendant depicted in Kooijman that 'resurfaced' during the past few yearly festivals, made by a man from Kokonau. Only once, for the first time and only time, a man brought me a bamboo penis sheath, such as those illustrated in Kooijman.

While not very artistic, we have seen some carved pigs several times at '*Karapao*' festivals in Kekwa Village. These pigs, some 30 to 40 cm. long, have offering of sago laid in front of them, along with miniature spears.

Sympathetic magic, undoubtedly, especially as I was told that this pig display helps the hunters find an abundance of wild pigs. (It does not always work...). None of these pig figures are in Kooijman's book.

Several new types of carvings have emerged during the last several years, aside from stand-alone animals. These include humans inside fish or crocodiles, elaborate sago bowls that look like fish (the traditional ones are quite plain by comparison) sometimes with a crab or other animal inside. Many human figures wearing spirit masks have appeared, due to their successful sales. One carver made an unusual item, showing human arms and legs, protruding from under a real turtle shell.

Choosing carvings for the yearly festival

During my purchasing trips for expositions/sales, it was easy to reject poor quality carvings. This did not hold true for the yearly Kamoro festival auctions where I tried to follow a general rule I set for myself: at least one carving per village. As being selected for the auctions automatically meant a high price, thus instant (relative) wealth for the carver, I tried to spread this as widely as possible. Not easy: some villages came up only with some quite awful carvings. I tried to pick the 'least bad' one, but occasionally I did not pick any and thus had to bear the ill-will of some carvers. During the first few years of the festival, I was the object of a great deal of resentment from carvers whose pieces I did not choose. My argument with them was that I knew what the potential buyers wanted. Eventually, most of the disappointed men stopped criticizing my choices, although I still have to put up with occasional grumbling bordering on the aggressive. Then, over the years, most Kamoro gave me their confidence in my impartiality. While I have many friends among them, I consciously refrain from allowing my friendships to influence my selection. Ditto for those Kamoro I dislike.

On the other side of the coin, some villages brought too many excellent carvings. Here I sometimes chose two (very occasionally three) carvings and, very seldom, two carvings by the same artist. I tried to always have the very best pieces for the auction but picked some lesser pieces to spread the money widely to dilute the overall quality of the carvings. In another compromise, I attempted to pick a variety of pieces, as for my exhibit/sales. And, as the time for the auctions was limited, I could pick only some 60-odd pieces each year.

Unfortunately, the number of buyers and their enthusiasm during these auctions were not always the same. The same piece could fetch three to five times more at one auction than another. In each auction, I picked the sequence of pieces to offer for bidding, trying not to pick two carvings of the same type one after another. If I saw that the enthusiasm was high, I attempted to move some of the lesser attractive carvings, interspersed with a few of the best ones. Thus, the timing of each piece which was picked and when, could greatly affect its price. That was the luck of the draw for the carvers.

The prices at the auction varied greatly, from about $30 to a high of $1,100. The average tended to be around $150 per piece. The men were free to sell any carvings they had brought to the festival, those I had not picked for the auction, were bought directly from them by the visitors.

The physical setup at the Kamoro festival helped me to make my choices. On the side of the large auction hall, a U-shaped raised walkway (necessary due to daily tidal flooding), extended about 60 meters on each of its three sides. The organizing committee had the local men from Pigapu Village build simple thatched shelters on each side of this walkway, with a front porch where the carvings were displayed for viewing.

I made several rounds of the walkway in order to choose my 50 to 60 carvings. This was because some of the participants do not arrive on the appointed day, some coming in as much as three days late. And while each village - with 25 official participants - can supposedly occupy only one of the shelters, the early arrivals, if numerous (over the 25-limit) often took up two or more of these shelters, forcing groups who arrive later to set up camp under tarps, anywhere where there was flat space. They displayed their carvings in front of these tarp-tents.

The participants were supposed to arrive one day before the official opening, so I started choosing from their carvings as soon as they were settled. On this first round, I picked very few pieces, as I knew many other groups have not yet arrived. It took a half-dozen rounds to pick all the carvings, some of which come in only a few hours before the auction started. Even if I had already picked a carving from a particular village on a previous round, I might select another one if I felt it was of top quality. I wanted to pick the very best carvings for the auction, balanced however with giving more carvers this opportunity.

While I made the rounds, I had an assistant or two for record-keeping purposes. We gave each selected carving a number and took a Polaroid photo of the carver and his carving. (This was before digital photography days.) On the record sheet and on the Polaroid, we wrote the name of the artist and his current village residence. If there was time, we added a short description of the carving. I also took photos: slides as well as color negatives for future reference. Our records from the various festivals are relatively complete. The lists are available from each year' auctions, thanks to my assistant, Luluk Intarti. There is only a gap for 1999, when she was pregnant and could not be present.

The buyers of the carvings were a disparate lot. They included Freeport personnel, government officials, an occasional dealer-collector and, most of all, wealthy guests of Freeport Indonesia, flown in by the company from Jakarta. The number of bidders at the auctions varied greatly: from a low of a half-dozen individuals, to a high of a couple of dozen.

Size matters. Most buyers of Kamoro art would not purchase pieces much above 2 meters high or long. This created a problem for selling full-sized 'mbitoro', which can reach some seven meters (and weigh well over 200 kg.). We sold only a few of these during the Kamoro festival, with most going to decorate the front of government buildings or the Freeport exploration office. (The large ironwood carvings seen in Kuala Kencana or in front of the Rimba (ex-Sheraton) Hotel were ordered by Freeport directly from Pak Timo Samin, before the yearly festivals began.)

For the Freeport guests at the yearly festival, shipping back to Jakarta presented no problems as the company took care of wrapping and shipping to the capital city. Other buyers had to take care of the shipping themselves. Many sent their carvings by airfreight to Bali, and then trans-shipped through an agent to their final destination. Of course, smaller and lighter pieces could be taken on the flight out of Timika as checked luggage, covered with the 'fragile' stickers.

Choosing carvings for exhibits/sales

My self-assigned job of picking the carvings for the auctions of the yearly Kamoro festival gave me an inordinate amount of power in shaping the direction of the evolution of Kamoro carvings. And this was in addition to my periodic buying trips when I selected pieces for upcoming expositions/sales that I organized in Bali, Surabaya, Jakarta, Tembagapura, Kuala Kencana and in Leiden, in The Netherlands, under the joint sponsorship of Freeport and the Rijksmuseum voor Volkenkunde. (See the Chapter 12 below.)

As my budgets from Freeport were limited, I could not travel to the Kamoro villages far from Timika. I purchased carvings from those groups that I could reach by road, or within a range of a couple of hours by canoe. For any particular selling event, I bought from 50 to some 100 new pieces after looking at several villages' displays of carvings. I purchased the items at a low price ($5 to $15) with the clear understanding that after the carving was sold (if it was sold) the artist would receive the lion's share of the profits, with a small percentage kept for expenses. So, for example if a *'yamate'* sold for $200, the carver would receive about $160 – that is the sale price minus the down payment and an administrative fee. The selling prices depended most of all on the kind of guest and the venue, their personal tastes (foreigners mostly but also some Indonesians too), and what there was on offer. Most sales prices ranged from $25 to $200, with more money generated at the occasional mini auction. While most carvers received a modest income from these sales, three or four of the best ones could receive well over $1,000 over the course of just one year.

On a typical buying trip, I would purchase carvings from about 60 individuals from 15 to 20 villages or settlements. In my opinion, these items ranged from good to excellent. While occasionally under pressure to buy poor quality pieces, I steadfastly refused: it was better for carvers without the necessary skills to stop carving and go out to fish or make sago to feed their families.

While some of the cash from the carvings was undoubtedly wasted on alcohol and prostitutes, the bulk of it went to family. And the money not only helped the carvers' immediate families, but also friends and relatives. It was always heartening to me when I gave a man a good-sized dollop of cash, to see him hand it over right away to his wife. It was then certain the money would not be wasted.

I had several aims when I select carvings. These aims sometimes came in conflict with one another. First, I had to buy pieces that would sell or I would end up with a large stock of carvings rotting in some warehouse. I wanted to give economic help to as many Kamoro carvers as possible, but buying un-saleable carvings is not a sustainable proposition. Those carvers who did not have the skills to make saleable pieces were wasting their time and were better off doing something else to feed their families: fishing, making sago, hunting, working at some paid job around Timika. While the Kamoro area is rich in natural resources, access to markets is a huge problem for those living far from the primary market of Timika and a secondary one at Kokonau. These men are cash-poor, with practically no way to earn the money necessary for school fees or what have now become necessities such as kerosene, salt, cigarettes, fuel and spare parts for outboard motors, axes and machetes.

After the demise of the festival I traveled to every Kamoro village at least once a year, but both time and resources were lacking for making more than a yearly trip to the furthest villages. Then, with my budget cut, this meant that most of my purchases covered less than half of the 60-odd villages or settlements, spread along 250 km of coast as well as a short distance inland.

Aside from pieces that would sell, I tried to encourage the continuation of traditional carvings as well as new, creative pieces. Problems of transportation and shipping precluded buying very large pieces such as normal, ritual-sized 'mbitoro', which are 5 or more meters high.

The Kamoro Art Gallery

We set up an art gallery in Timika to help with individual sales of Kamoro carvings and other items, including Asmat and Sempan collections. The location was in the house where my assistant Luluk Intarti lived, first near central Timika, then in the southern part of town when she moved there. At this second location, we built a special large room next to Luluk's house to serve as our gallery.

A few Indonesians from town occasionally came by and even bought a piece, but most of our clients were Freeport employees, or rather their wives when they were brave enough to visit Timika. They usually did this in small groups, as they did not speak Indonesian and were afraid of what could happen to them in town. Few of them were courageous enough to leave the safe confines of the Freeport-controlled areas. Occasionally a husband-and-wife team from the company highlands town of Tembagapura would come to the gallery and purchase several items when they were ready to return to the US at the end of their contract.

We always kept a large selection of items, all with very reasonable prices. Luluk, who spoke good English, would allow a bit bargaining, but the expatriates usually paid the asking price. Outside of the gallery, we kept a few very large human figures carved in hard ironwood. A government official might buy several of them for his office or an expatriate who wanted to take them home thanks to free shipping by Freeport.

Often Kamoro carvers come to where I was living in Timika to sell me one or more pieces. I bought only a few of these, as the gallery was usually well stocked. The carvers would then sell their other items to one of several souvenir shops on one of Timika's main streets. Of course, these shops would pay a very low price but at least the carver did not have to return home without any money. The Bugis-run souvenir shops were our main competitors in town. They specialized in the most common Papuan souvenirs, such as the highlands penis sheaths, often over-decorated with fanciful, non-traditional designs. We kept to better quality genuine art items.

The Kamoro team in Leiden poses in front of the large poster erected to announce the Rijksmuseum's Kamoro exhibit. Translated from the Dutch, the poster has in large yellow letters: Papua Lives! Underneath the white letters say: Meet the Kamoro. The Kamoro participated in the exhibit for almost three weeks.

TAKING CARVERS OUT OF WEST NEW GUINEA

12

The Kamoro participants pose in traditional Dutch dress, with accessories. After each person received a copy of the photo, they returned to their housing where every time they looked at the photo it brought forth uncontrolled laughter.

I invited several Kamoro carvers to enliven the various exhibitions/sales held in Bali, Surabaya and Jakarta or for Freeport employees in West New Guinea, at the company towns of Kuala Kencana and Tembagapura. Due to a limited budget, I could only ask five or six men to travel to a venue outside of New Guinea. Airfast, an airline under contract to Freeport, flew us, along with the carvings, with no charges to our destination. In the '*outer world*' the Kamoro began learning about how things were different from their village. For many, it was their first trip in an airplane. I always tried to invite at least one Kamoro who had never flown before, and asked the others to explain to how to use the toilet, how to eat out of a tray or ask for a drink. This learning was repeated on arrival at our accommodation: how to use the bathing facilities, and especially the toilet (*no* to squatting on the toilet seat!)

Arriving at our destination, the carvers would help to set up the pieces in the venue allotted to us. This could be the auditorium of a school, several rooms in the home of an ambassador, a shopping center or a large hall at the American Club in Jakarta. Each item was tagged with an identification number, the name of the carver, his village, the type of object and the price in rupiahs. This went along with a 'certificate of authenticity' guaranteeing the item was a genuine Kamoro tribal product, signed by myself. And that is was *not* made in Bali!

During the exhibit, the Kamoro wore their traditional clothing, as did myself. The men would carve small pieces and when I signalled, they played the drums and danced. The visitors took photos or posed with the Kamoro for snapshots. While each carving was priced for most of the sales, at the American Club and some Embassies, we were able to hold silent auctions which allowed guests to come early and select the pieces they wanted. Each guest was given a purchase card on which they wrote the name of the carver, serial number and price of the carving. On the identification card of the carving they wrote their name and put on a red sticker to indicate that it was sold. At any time in the evening, the guest could take the purchase card to the cashier and complete his or her purchase by paying for everything in cash. This created a very exciting mood in the room and the carvers would happily carry the sold carvings out with the new owners as they could see immediately that they were getting their '*hasil*' (harvest).

We wanted to take advantage of these trips to show the Kamoro the wider world. They were suitably impressed and had many tales to share with their fellows once back in West New Guinea. Sometimes, they were overwhelmed into silence. Shopping was always a priority on their agenda after the carvings they made had been sold. Prices for clothing, household items, shoes, watches, sunglasses, and toys were considerably cheaper in Jakarta than back home in Timika. Traffic jams were a wonder everywhere, especially in Jakarta. Elevated streets and toll roads were also impressive. In Jakarta, we took them to the excellent Rangunan city zoo where the tame orangutans were the biggest hit. They also saw Tanjung Priok port area, a beehive of activity of loading and unloading of the '*pinisi*', traditional wooden ships, very different from their own tree-log canoes. Monas, the imposing independence monument topped with a huge golden flame was probably their first elevator ride to the top for super-wide panoramic views of the capital.

In Surabaya, we took the group to a '*kretek*' factory where clove-infused cigarettes (that all the Kamoro smoked) were, on an old factory floor, still hand-rolled on the thighs of the women who worked there. From Surabaya we also traveled some six hours by mini-bus to the town of Jepara for an overnight stay. In Jepara, we visited its large carving area, with many shops that combined into one main Javanese carving center. The Kamoro watched as large blocks of wood were quickly sculpted into traditional shapes, admiring the speed of the work as well as the handling of steel tools. On a far smaller scale, this was even more impressive in Bali, where Balinese and Kamoro carving groups joined to make different items were made. And the Kamoro men were most appreciative of the fine tools used by the Balinese carvers. When finances permitted, I bought sets of Balinese carving tools that I gave to some of the best Kamoro carvers. The tools resulted in finer detailed work than anything done previously. Bali also showed the Kamoro perhaps the best example of a culture where ancient traditions were maintained while stepping into the modern world at the same time.

Our most successful programs were held in various schools where the Kamoro taught the pupils some of their traditional skills. This started with carvings, where the students (depending on age) hit the chisel held by a Kamoro, while the older ones carved a Kamoro motif into a block of softwood. Often, a Kamoro would help several children with completing a simple design, finishing off with a smooth polish with sandpaper. The kids would then pose proudly with their work and the Kamoro teacher clad in his traditional clothes. Learning to beat drums was even more fun. First learned was the handling and striking of a single drum, then the beating of several drums in sync with one another. Some of the older kids became quite good at this exercise. Best of all, the Kamoro taught dancing to a whole class who would then perform outdoors amidst shouts and lots of laughing. In some schools, we ended our program with the kids and the Kamoro performing in a special assembly for the parents who became very willing buyers of our carvings.

The Kamoro exposition in Holland

Thanks to invitations from Freeport, Karen Jacobs, an anthropologist from Belgium, Herman de Boer a cameraman from Leiden and Dirk Smidt, the curator of the Department of Oceania in the Rijksmuseum voor Volkenkunde (The National Museum of Ethnography) in Leiden (The Netherlands) attended several of the yearly Kamoro festivals. Karen was there in 2000, 2001, 2002, and 2005 while Dirk was present in 2000 and 2002 and Herman de Boer in 2002. These visits fit in very well with a planned Kamoro exhibit at the Leiden Ethnography Museum that ran from February to August 2003. And to liven up their exhibit, Dirk Smidt invited some Kamoro to participate by traveling from Indonesia to Leiden. It was up to me to pick who would attend, choosing two women and three male carvers. I picked Kamoro who had experience traveling by airplane inside Indonesia, knew about western toilet facilities, and who were not prone to overdoing their alcohol consumption.

Taking these factors into consideration, I chose Timo Samin and his wife Modesta, Martinus Neyakowau, Yopi Kunareyao, and Mathea Mamoyau. A cameraman from Freeport filmed these selected participants in their home settings and their departure from Timika, as the Leiden museum planned to produce a video on their visit to Holland.

Picking the Kamoro was the easy part. Then came the difficult problems: obtaining first passports, then visas for them. For passports, we needed police recommendations of good behavior (no criminal acts) and letters of recommendation from village chiefs and other government officials. Looking back on our efforts, I can easily call it a bureaucratic nightmare. The time 'wasted ' was phenomenal. But what followed was worse: obtaining a visa for Holland, a part of the pan-European Community Schengen visa zone. Endless forms had to be filled out and presented in person by the Kamoro along with the letters of recommendation from Freeport and the Leiden Rijksmuseum. I was not allowed to enter the Dutch consulate in Jakarta and the Kamoro had to fend for themselves in oral interviews (conducted by Indonesians) where they were asked many questions they could not answer. We hoped for the best when we returned to Timika. After some ten days I got the bad news: the visa applications were rejected. International calls from Timika to Holland were not easy, as I tried to contact the Leiden Museum to ask what to do about our plight. Finally, my wife Jina got through to the museum in Leiden from Singapore. It took an important museum official phoning a personal friend in the Dutch ministry of foreign affairs... who then phoned the consulate in Jakarta to tell the underlings there to issue visas pronto for our team of Kamoro. This was in the nick of time, as we almost missed our scheduled flight to Holland.

After finally landing in The Netherlands, my stress level dropped considerably as the Leiden Ethnographic Museum took us under its welcoming wings. Dirk Smidt and Herman de Boer (who had filmed the 2002 Kamoro festival in Pigapu) met us on arrival, From that point on, Herman was never without his camera as every stage of the Kamoro's visit was captured on film. We traveled in two packed minibuses from Amsterdam's Schiphol Airport some 50 kilometers to the Rijksmuseum in Leiden. Our accommodations were in a clean and spacious building, with modern facilities, located in the museum complex. In front of the museum, a small peaceful canal was filled with fat geese. Our Kamoro men right away wanted to capture the birds for our evening meal.... I had to explain that these birds were definitely off-limits to hunting, were public property and lived for the viewing pleasure of the Dutch people.

An emotional visit

Later on our first day, Dirk Smidt took our group on a tour of the Kamoro displays at the museum. We saw many ancient carvings next to newly created ones Dirk had purchased at the auctions, as he wanted to show how the Kamoro art had survived and evolved somewhat. Herman was filming the visit when we saw a '*mbitoro*' that had been collected by Jan Pouwer in the early 1950s. Mathea reacted first, feeling faint and needing to sit. She told us later that she had seen her ancestors in the '*mbitoro*' that was displayed! She began crying and we took her outside, cutting short the visit. Once outside,

Timo began crying too, and as I tried to comfort him, began crying myself in sympathy (I cry easily...). Soon everyone was fighting back tears while the filming continued.

Herman asked me what was going on, as he could not understand Indonesian and did not know just why we were all so emotional. I told him: 'For the Kamoro, this totem pole is not a museum piece. They felt and saw their ancestors in the '*mbitoro*'... this was about meeting their ancestral past. They sensed spiritual beings, not an old carving. This totem pole is a vital piece from their past.' Timo added as I translated for Herman who kept filming: 'This carving could not have been kept back home in West New Guinea... it has been so many generations (over 150 years) in this museum... first time we saw such old ancestral carvings; we are grateful that this piece had been preserved. We know now what high values the Dutch people placed on this ancestral piece because they collected it and kept it for so long. And we are very grateful to Ibu Jina and Pak Kal for having brought us here, to meet our ancestors.' (Jacobs, 2011)

That night on Timo's suggestion and with his directions, we set offerings on a table outdoors for the ancestors to show our gratefulness for their presence. This included Indonesian rupiahs and kretek (clove) cigarettes. The next morning, we saw that the night wind had scattered our presents. Timo said this showed their ancestors had accepted the offerings.

Daily activities

While the Kamoro exhibit had started in February and was to run for six months, the museum management wanted to take advantage of the Kamoro's presence to attract a wider public. Our team stayed in Holland from 18 May to 5 June. The museum advertised its presence with press releases and large posters stating: Papua Leeft! Ontmoet de Kamoro (Dutch for: 'Papua Lives! Meet the Kamoro').

Our group was given a raised stage in the museum's foyer where the men carved and the ladies made items from plaited grass. We had an initial problem in locating a source of wood for carvings, not too hard and not too soft. After trying several kinds of Dutch wood, the men picked one that was suitable. After visiting a Dutch carver, the men wanted to purchase the same set of tools they had seen. These were horrendously expensive, so they had to be satisfied with only a few special steel European chisels.

We had brought several drums, and when we had a good-sized audience, Timo would start playing and the rest would spontaneously start dancing. As Dutch visitors were looking on, they were invited to dance. Some were too shy to participate, but others joined enthusiastically creating a friendly ambience. Martinus had brought an unusual instrument that neither Jina or I had ever seen before. It was a kind of a rattle made of bamboo. Because it was a sacred instrument, Martinus would always turn his body away to play it and then immediately hide it from view. After the first week when it became increasingly difficult for him to stay in that awkward position, Timo gave him permission to reveal to everyone. It was a bamboo section of about meter long with a vertical cut about three cm wide. A long mat of thin rattan strips roughly spaced apart was rolled up to fit tightly into the bamboo section. By pulling a string attached to the mat and releasing it from its holder quickly, one could produce a loud rattling sound to accompany the drumming.

Not all visitors were able to watch the demonstration of the Kamoro's traditional way to fasten the lizard skin on top of the drum. This required fresh human blood to act as glue. Before the demonstration, I described the upcoming process and warned the members of the Dutch public that one of us was going to donate the necessary blood, obtained by small razor cuts to the calf. Several of the squeamish public left at this stage. Herman duly filmed the demonstration.

The visitors included some Dutch people who had lived in Dutch East New Guinea, other Indonesians like Moluccans and a number of Papuans living in Holland. Some of the latter had self-exiled when the European colonists were forced to leave West New Guinea under the combined diplomatic pressure from the US and Indonesian military attacks (largely ineffectual) in the 1960s. They had been living in Holland so long they had practically forgotten their Indonesian language. They were still set against the Jakarta government and were disappointed when the Kamoro did not show any anti-Indonesian attitudes.

Jean-Jacques Dozy was the Dutch geologist who had been a member of the three-man Dutch team in 1936 to reach the highest central mountains and discover what became Freeport's Ertsberg mine. I had interviewed him several years beforehand while researching a book about Freeport. He was still a spry old gentleman as was another visitor, Jan Pouwer, the anthropologist who had studied the Kamoro in the 1950s. When the Kamoro learned that Dr. Pouwer was coming, they formed a welcoming committee to greet him outside our 'house' and walk with him as an honor escort while dancing and playing the drums.

The museum provided each of us with a €30 daily stipend for our meals. I handled the budget for everyone so that at the end of trip there would be shopping money and a good saving of the stipend that could be taken home. I gave my wife a daily budget for all our three meals which she would prepare except for Tuesdays when the museum closed and the Kamoro would be taken on tours. She would trudge to a nearby supermarket each day to buy rice and other groceries that she cooked in the kitchen facilities of our accommodations. A lot of work for her, preparing lunch and dinner, but she used up only about a third of our allowance, saving each Kamoro a nice chunk of change. With several hundred euros per person put aside from the food budget, plus earnings from whatever items the Kamoro made and sold, each was able to apply the euros to their shopping.

The museum staff drove us around Holland so that the Kamoro could see some of the country aside from the insides of the Rijksmuseum. We drove along the road on top of some of the fantastic system of dykes that greatly increased the size of the nation, but that made no impression on our Kamoro. Nor did the many Dutch people ride bicycles. But then, driving along a quiet street one day, we saw a man with several dogs of different sizes and breeds on leashes. I explained that this man was being paid by the owners of the dogs to walk them around every day. The Kamoro found this nearly beyond belief. They asked to stop and to be photographed with the man and the pooches. That dogs needed a paid man to walk them daily was perhaps the most incredible thing they saw in Holland. The most humorous event was their trip to Voldendam where they got to dress in traditional Dutch clothing and pose for a group photo. Back at our museum accommodations, the photos were looked at over and over amidst uncontrolled hilarity as they grabbed each other, even rolling on the floor, laughing endlessly.

Carvings and an auction

Before leaving Timika, I sent a shipment of carvings to the Rijksmuseum with Freeport helping with the packing and paying all charges. The items included a very unusual '*mbitoro*' from Iwaka. It's wing projection held some 50 human figures, each one representing someone from the village who had

At the beginning of the auction, the Kamoro men and myself posed with the director of the Rijksmuseum. Many items were sold and the Kamoro used their euros to shop in Holland before returning home.

died (men, women, children) since the previous initiation. This was such an unusual carving that I bought it for about $1,000 and wanted the museum to own and display this unique item. As it would have been impossible to ship this '*mbitoro*' with the wing attached, it was carefully cut off, then dowels and holes made for reassembly after it had arrived.

Along with the '*mbitoro*' I sent about 100 carvings for potential sale in Holland. Before we had arrived, the shipment had already landed at the museum, but everything had to be put into freezer storage for three weeks to kill all the wood-boring beasts before the carvings were allowed into tropical-bug-free Holland. Once we checked out the shipment (the '*mbitoro*' survived splendidly), I offered to Dirk Smidt and the museum any carvings he wanted (he took about a dozen) and we set up the rest for an auction. This was held at the museum, with the Dutch public invited to attend and participate.

The team and I put on traditional Kamoro dress and accoutrements. As we were getting ready, they were joking around in Indonesian as though we were already selling the items: '*tambah, tambah!*' (more, more!); '*seratus euro*'! (one hundred euros) '*lebih!*' (more!), '*seratus lima puluh!*' (one hundred and fifty!). As we entered the hall in the museum where the auction was to take place, our men beat drums and we were all dancing and singing. The audience included some missionaries who had served many years among the Kamoro and some nuns. In fact, afterwards, Mathea met a nun who had been one of her teachers in Kokonau before the Dutch were forced to leave in 1963, forty years previously. (Jacobs, 2011)

After our entry, I made a short speech to announce how I was going to conduct the auction (in English) that was to benefit the Kamoro. Aside from the pieces I had sent from Timika, the auction now included items the Kamoro had made while in Leiden. I began the auction by selecting an item, giving it to Timo to show to the audience while the other two men softly played the drums and the women danced. I then started with a low bid and waited until someone topped that amount... as in any auction. As the price rose, the drumming became more intense. At the final bid, when the price would go no higher, I called it sold! And the Kamoro and the audience applauded. On to the next item. The auction ended up selling a total of 64 carvings for a total of €6,430. Later, on other days, we conducted further sales to individual buyers, with 73 more items bringing in about €7,000. A small portion went to the museum with the bulk of the money divided evenly among the Kamoro team.

The end of the Leiden Kamoro exposition: disappointments

The Kamoro team spent most of their good-sized chunk of euros in shopping. Good quality suitcases topped the items, followed by clothes, watches and toys. Over the weeks and continued publicity in the newspapers had made the Kamoro famous in Leiden, so in some shops they even got free shoes and new reading glasses. The team returned to Indonesia in a happy mood.

For me, it was the opposite. Although I was happy that the Kamoro had a wonderful experience in Europe and left with piles of purchases, I was disappointed with the Rijksmuseum's unfulfilled promises. Dirk Smidt failed to acknowledge the receipt of the unique '*mbitoro*' I had donated to the museum (with Freeport's essential participation). As far as I know, it went into long-term storage and was never mentioned.

Then the video of the Kamoro visit was never completed. While Herman de Boer requested to copy the tape of what Jina had filmed in the Netherlands, we never got our tape back. Nor did Herman share the filming of the emotional scene of when the Kamoro saw the '*mbitoro*' collected by Jan Pouwer. The museum's next exposition, Tintin in Peru became the focus just as the Kamoro left. All the films shot in our participation have been destined for oblivion. After I returned to West New Guinea, my emails to Herman de Boer, Dirk Smidt as well as the director of the Rijksmuseum went unanswered.

BIBLIOGRAPHY

[UABS = Universitas Cenderawasih and Australian University Baseline Study]

Barrau, J. 1959. The sago & other food plants of marsh dwellers South Pacific Islands. *Economic Botany* 13:151-62.

Boelaars, M. S. C. 1971. The Auwju People. In: F. Trenkenschuh. *An Asmat Sketchbook #3*, Crosier Missions, Hastings, Nebraska, USA. pp. 41-74.

Boelaars, M. S. C. 1971. The Jaquai People. In: F. Trenkenschuh. *An Asmat Sketchbook #3*, Crosier Missions, Hastings, Nebraska, USA. pp. 7-40.

Boelaars, J. H. M. C. 1981. Head-Hunters About Themselves. *Verhandelingen van het Koninklijk Instituut voor Taal-, Land-, en Volkenkunde*. (92). Martinus Nijhoff, The Hague.

Boelaars, JHC. 1950. *The Linguistic Position of South West New Guinea*. Brill, Leiden.

Corbey, R. 1993. *Ethnographic Showcases, 1870-1930*. Cultural Anthropology 8(3): 338-369.

Ellen, R. F. 1986. Conundrums about panjandrums: on the use of titles in the relations of Political subordination in the Moluccas and along the Papuan Coast. *Indonesia* 41: 47-62.

Herdt, Gilbert H. 1993. *Ritualized Homosexuality in Melanesia*. University California Press, Berkeley.

Kamma, F. C. and S. Kooijman. 1973. *Romawa Forja Child of Fire*. Brill, Leiden.

Knauft, Bruce 1993. *South Coast New Guinea Cultures*. Cambridge University Press.

Leith, D. 2003. *The Politics of Power. Freeport in Suharto's Indonesia*. University of Hawai'i Press, Honolulu.

Marshall, A. and B. Beehler. 2007. *The Ecology of Papua*. Periplus Editions, Singapore.

Mealey, G. 1996. *Grasberg.* Freeport-Mac-Mo-Ran Copper and Gold Inc, Singapore.

Menzies, E. 2009. *Papua.* Hexart Publishing, Jakarta.

Moore, Clive. 2004. *Crossing Boundaries and History.* University of Hawai'i Press.

Muller, K. 1991. *Indonesian New Guinea.* Periplus Editions, Singapore.

Muller, K. 2005. *Keragaman Hayati Tanah Papua.* [Biodiversity of New Guinea] Universitas Negeri Papua, Manokwari. ISBN 979-97700-5-X.

Muller, K. n.d. *Exploring Mimika (1828-1973)* unpublished text

Paijmans, K. (ed.) 1976. *New Guinea.* Australian National University Press, Canberra.

Pawley, A. (et al, eds.) 2005. *Papuan Pasts.* Australian National University, Canberra.

Roder, J. 1956. The Rock Paintings of the MacCluer Bay. *Antiquity and Survival* 5 pp. 387-400.

Ruddle, Kenneth (et al. eds.) 1978. *Palm Sago. A Tropical Starch from Marginal Lands.* University of Hawaii, East-West Center.

Ryan, P. (ed.) 1972. *Encyclopaedia of Papua and New Guinea.* Melbourne: Melbourne University Press.

Rhys, L. 1947. *Jungle Pimpernel.* Hodder and Stoughton, London.

Serpenti, L. M. 1977. *Cultivators in the Swamps.* Van Gorcum, Assen, The Netherlands.

Sillitoe, Paul. 1998. *An Introduction to the Anthropology of Melanesia.* Cambridge University Press.

Silzer, P. 1991. *Index of Irian Jaya Languages.* Summer Institute of Linguistics. Jayapura.

Smedts, M. 1955. *No Tobacco, No Hallelujah.* William Kimber, London.

Verslag Militaire Exploratie 1920. Verslag van de Militaire Exploratie van der Nederlandsch-Nieuw-Guinee, 1907-1915. Landsdrukkerij, Welterden.

Young, Michael. 1985. Abutu in Kalauna: a retrospect. *Mankind,* 15:2.

SPECIFICALLY KAMORO BIBLIOGRAPHY

Ballard, C. et al. 1997. *An Annotated Bibliography for the Kamoro People.* UNCEN-ANU Baseline Studies Project. Canberra

Bijlmer, H.J.T. 1939. Tapiro pygmies and Paniai mountain-Papuans: results of the Anthropological Mimika Expedition in New Guinea, 1935–36. *Nova Guinea* (n.s.) 3: 113–184.

Coenen, J. 1963. Beberapa aspek kebudayaan rohani daerah Mimika. Unpublished manuscript.

Coenen, J. 2010. *Kamoro: Aspek-aspek Kebudayaan Asli.* Indonesian translation of J. Coenen's 1963 Enkele Facetten van de Geestelijke Cultuur van de Mimika by Father F. Hoogenboom. Kansius ,Yogyakarta.

Drabbe, Peter, 1953. *Spraakkunst van de Kamoro-taal / door.* M. Nijhoff, s'Gravenhage.

Drabbe, Petrus, m.s.c. 1947–1950. Folk-tales from Netherlands New Guinea. *Oceania* 18(2):157–175, (3):248–270; 19(1):75–90, (3):224–240.

Earl, George Windsor 1853. The Native Races of the Indian Archipelago. *Papuans.* Hippolyte Bailliere, London.

Earl, G. W. 1837. "Narrative of a voyage along the southwest coast of New Guinea, in 1828, and communicated by G. Windsor Earl." *Journal of the Royal Geographical Society* (London) 7 : 385–395. (This is an account of the Triton expedition of 1828.)

Haddon, Alfred C. (Alfred Court, 1855–1940). 1916. *Report made by the Wollaston Expedition on the ethnographical collections from the Utakwa River, Dutch New Guinea.* London.

Harple, Todd. 2000. *Controlling the Dragon: An ethnohistorical analysis of the Kamoro of South-West New Guinea.* PhD. Dissertation Australian National University, Canberra.

Jacobs, K. 2007. Kamoro Kakuru: the Kamoro Festival in Pigapu, Papua. In: *Representing Pacific Art*, eds. K. Stevenson and V. Lee-Webb, pp. 91-110. University of Hawai'i Press, Honolulu.

Jacobs, Karen. 2003. Collecting Kamoro. PhD. Dissertation. University of East Anglia.

Jacobs, K. and D. Smidt 2003. *Kamoro Masks*. Digital publication from the National Museum of Ethnology, Leiden.

Kamoro Baseline Study. 1998 *UABS Report #7. Final Report Kamoro Baseline Study*. UNCEN-ANU Baseline Studies Project, Canberra.

Kolff, Dirk Hendrik, 1840. *Voyages of the Dutch Brig of War Dourga*. J. Madden, London.

Kooijman, S. 1984. *Art, Art Objects, and Ritual in the Mimika Culture*. Brill, Leiden.

Lagerborg, Mary Ann 1994. *Incessant Drumbeat. Trial and Triumph in Irian Jaya*. Christian Literature Crusade, Fort Washington, Pennsylvania.

Miklouho-Maclay, N. 1982. *Travels to New Guinea*. Progress Publishers, Moscow.

Meek, A.S. (Alexander, b. 1865) 1913. *A naturalist in Cannibal Land*. Ed. Frank Fox, with an introduction by the Hon. Walter Rothschild, and thirty-six illustrations. T.F. Unwin, London, Leipsic.

Muller, Kal c. 2012. WW II On the South Coast of Papua. Unpublished text.

Muller, Kal. N.d. Exploring Mimika. Unpublished text. Papuaweb.

Muller, Kal. 2000. *Kamoro Resources*. Unpublished book, Papuweb.

Muller, S. 1857. Reizen en onderzoekingen in den Indischen archipel gedaan op last der Nederlandsche Indiche regering, tusschen de jaren 1828 en 1836. F. Muller, Amsterdam.

Offenberg, G.A.M and Jan Pouwer (eds.) 2002. *Amoko. In the Beginning. Myths and Legends of the Asmat and Mimika Papuans*. Crawford House Australia Publishing, Adelaide.

Pickell, D. 2001. *Kamoro. Life Between the Tides*. Aopao Production, Indonesia.

Pouwer, Jan. 1955. *Enkele Aspecten van de Mimika-Cultuur*. Staatsdrukkenerij-en Uitgeversbedrijf, 'sGravenhave.

SPECIFICALLY KAMORO BIBLIOGRAPHY | 171

Pouwer, Jan. 1956. A Masquerade in Mimika. *Antiquity and Survival* 5:373-386.

Pouwer, Jan. 1999. The colonization, decolonization, and recolonization of West New Guinea. *Journal of Pacific History* 34(2): 157-179.

Pouwer, Jan. 2003. Kamoro life and ritual pp. 23-57 In D. Smidt (ed.) *Kamoro Art*. KIT Publishers, Amsterdam.

Pouwer, Jan. 2010. *Gender, Social formation and the ritual cycle in West-Papua. A configurational analysis comparative analysis comparing Kamoro and Asmat*. KITLV Press, Leiden.

Purba, T. et al. 1998. *Kamoro Phrase Book*. Universitas Cenderawasih, Jayapura.

Rawling, C. 1911. Explorations in Dutch New Guinea. *Geographical Journal* 38(3): 233-255.

Rawling, C. 1913. *The Land of the New Guinea Pygmies*. Seeley Service, London.

Smidt, Dirk. (ed.) 2003. *Kamoro Art*. KIT Publishers, Amsterdam.

Swadling, Pamela. 1996. *Plumes from Paradise*. Boroko and Coorparoo, Queensland. Papua New Guinea National Museum in Association with Robert Brown and Associated, Queensland.

Trenkenschuh, F. (ed.) 1982. *An Asmat Sketchbook* No. 1 & 2. Crosier Missions, Nebraska.

Webster, Herbert Cayley 1898. *Through New Guinea and the cannibal countries*. T. F. Unwin, London. [Chapter VII describes a violent encounter with possible Kamoro communities in Etna Bay]

Wollaston, Alexander 1912. *Pygmies and Papuans*. Smith, Elder, London.

Zee, P. van der. 2009. *Art as contact with the ancestors. The visual arts of the Kamoro and Asmat of Western Papua*. KIT Publishers, Amsterdam.

Zegwaard, G. A. 1995. The induction ritual and body decoration or recently initiated Young men in the Mimika Region. In: Dirk Smidt et al (eds.) *Pacific Material Culture*. Rijksmuseum voor Volkenkunde, Leiden pp. 308-323.

NOTE: Three videos by Georjina Chia Muller: Kamoro Carvers of Papua - The Biro, The Drum and The Canoe in Dutch, English and Bahasa Indonesia. Commissioned by the Rijksmuseum voor Volkenkunde, Leiden 2003.

Printed in the USA
CPSIA information can be obtained
at www.ICGtesting.com
LVHW021059200624
783492LV00004B/358